Baby Crafts

ROCKPORT

Baby Crafts

Unique Gifts for New Arrivals

GLOUCESTER MASSACHUSETTS

ROCKPORT PUBLISHERS

Lynne Farris

First published in the United States of America by
Rockport Publishers, Inc.
33 Commercial Street
Gloucester, Massachusetts 01930-5089

Telephone: (978) 282-9590
Facsimile: (978) 283-2742
www.rockpub.com

ISBN 1-56496-796-4

10 9 8 7 6 5 4 3 2 1

Design and Layout: *tabula rasa* graphic design

Cover Design: Jeannet Leendertse
Cover Image: Bobbie Bush Photography

Photography: Brian Piper Photography, West Chester, Pennsylvania,
except pages 15, 18 (bottom three photos), 19, 20, 21 by Michael
Lafferty; pages 22, 58 by Paul Whicheloe; page 40 courtesy of
Anna French, 0207-351-1126, www.annafrench.co.uk; page 76
by Corbis Stock Market

Printed in China.

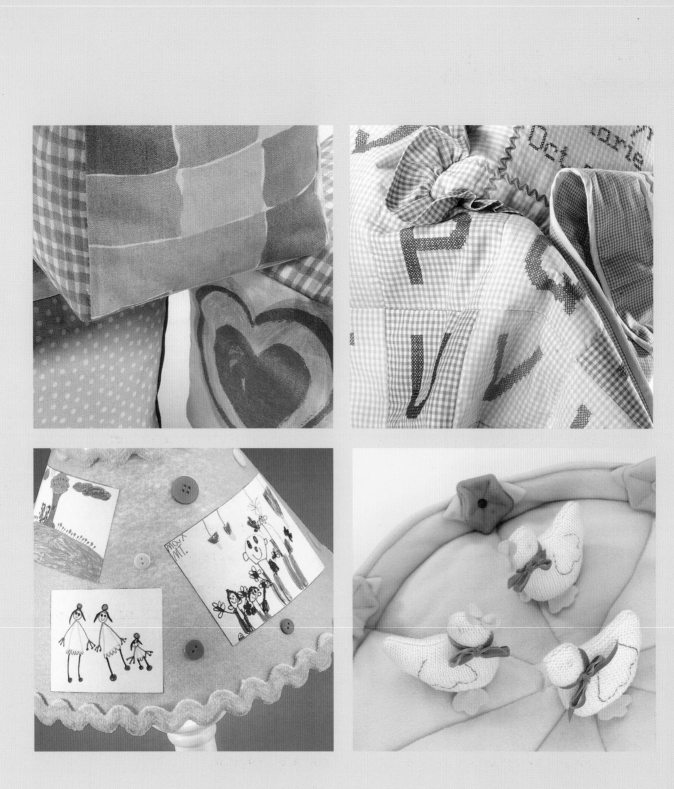

Contents

Introduction

IF YOU ARE READING THIS BOOK, *it's likely that you or perhaps someone close to you—a sister, a daughter or daughter-in-law, a cousin, an aunt, a friend, a coworker—is expecting a new baby. What an exciting time for friends and family to savor, in anticipation of the miracle that's taking place! It is only natural that you want to share in the celebration of this new life by creating handmade gifts that will become tomorrow's treasured keepsakes.*

While catalogs and specialty stores offer an endless supply of items designed with baby and mother in mind, nothing is quite so special as a gift you make with your own hands. You can choose the perfect color, style, and theme to coordinate with the baby's nursery. Or you might start a gift project now and personalize it after the baby arrives by adding her name or handprint to complete the design. You can even organize a creative baby shower where all the guests get together to make items for the new arrival.

One of the easiest ways to ensure the success of your project is to start with something purchased, such as a piece of clothing, a tote bag, or a basic toy, and then add embellishments to give it a personal touch. Or concentrate on making everyday items more meaningful. Photographs, for example, can be incorporated into handmade albums to capture those fleeting moments of wonder as baby grows and changes from day to day.

Whatever your interests and abilities, from sewing and knitting to painting and paper crafts, the projects assembled here offer a variety of creative gifts to make for the little one. Once you try some of the more basic projects, you might even be inspired to learn a new skill.

The book is divided into four main project sections: Baby's Room, Baby's Clothes and Comforts, Baby's Toys, and Baby's Memories. You will find a list of materials, suggestions and safety tips, helpful hints and shortcuts, as well as fully illustrated step-by-step instructions for each of the projects. There are also ideas for varying the projects to suit your personal style or that of the mom-to-be. A gallery section, called Baby's Delights, features eight additional project ideas to inspire you further. All the project materials are easy to find at fabric and craft stores, but if you need help or want further information on a product that's used, consult the resource guide at the back of the book.

Enjoy!

Crafter's Know-How

An Overview

THIS SECTION COVERS VARIOUS CRAFTING *techniques and materials. It will help you get started on the projects in this book and will also serve as a stepping stone to other crafting ideas and projects. You will find guides to choosing the right materials, explanations of various methods, and design and construction tips to assure the success of your projects. The know-how section is organized into three areas: the first covers sewing, needlework, and image transfer; the second covers knitting; and the third, paper crafting. Read through the appropriate section before embarking on your chosen project to make sure that you are familiar with the unique shortcuts, materials, and techniques presented here.*

Sewing, Needlework, and Image Transfer

Fabric Selection

The best fabrics to use for babies are woven fabrics, such as denim-weave cottons and crisp cotton blends, and knits, such as stretch terry cloth, T-shirt knits, and the fluffy fleece fabrics that are so popular today. You can usually find a superb selection at your local fabric retailer, but if not, or if your shopping time is limited, take advantage of an on-line fabric retailer (see resource guide) for speedy delivery of great fabrics right to your door. For truly personal fabric selection, you might even consider recycling part of a used accessory or garment, as we did for the Sweater Duck Family (page 60).

It is especially important when sewing for a baby that you prewash all fabrics, including previously used ones, before beginning your project. Prewashing removes any sizing or harsh chemicals, lets you check for colorfastness, and prevents shrinkage of the finished project. Following are some other items to consider.

Color

Don't be afraid to select unusual hues and color combinations. Babies respond to vibrant contrasts and can more easily focus on strong colors. Most of the information a baby gets about his environment in the first few months of life comes from the sense of sight.

Texture

Different textures help a baby get acquainted with the environment through the sense of touch. The contrast between a crisp, smooth cotton and a soft, fluffy fleece fabric will provide pleasurable sensations to a baby's sensitive and curious fingers.

Pattern

Both woven patterns, such as stripes and plaids, and printed patterns can enrich the surface of your work. The size of a printed pattern should be in keeping with the overall scale of the project. Highly contrasting and colorful patterns can be quite stimulating to the baby.

Weight

The weight of a fabric is determined by the closeness of the weave or knit as well as the thickness of the fibers themselves. If additional body or weight is needed, the fabric can be fused to another, more sturdy fabric, or backed with an interfacing.

Grain/Stretch

Pay attention to the grain of the fabric when laying out pattern pieces. Cutting off-grain can produce inferior results. To increase the amount of stretch in a woven fabric, cut on the bias, or diagonal to the grain. When working with knits, always take into account the amount of stretch that's likely or possible. Using a very stretchy fabric can increase the size of a stuffed piece by two to three times. To minimize stretch, apply fusible tricot stabilizer to the wrong side.

Thread

All-purpose polyester sewing threads are appropriate for most of the projects in this book. In certain cases, specialized heavy-duty threads, such as upholstery or hand-quilting threads, or even dental floss, may be suggested instead because they are stronger or make an item safer for baby. For surface embellishment, use cotton or rayon embroidery floss, or even yarn. These offer colorful options for creating details such as facial features on stuffed animals.

Cutting and Construction

The sewing projects in this book take advantage of several innovative sewing and cutting techniques that, when used correctly, make it easy to get excellent results. If you are an experienced sewer, some of the instructions may appear to be putting the cart before the horse. In fact, you may be tempted to jump right in and correct our mistakes—after all, who ever would sew before cutting out? There is, however, a method to this madness. Be sure to read all project instructions completely before cutting into your fabric.

Three basic construction methods are used.

Sew First, Cut Later

One shortcut for creating basic two-layer shapes—that is, where the front and back are exactly the same—is to cut a template to the exact shape and size of the finished piece, without adding the seam allowance. The template is placed on the fabric and an air-soluble marking pen is used to trace around it. With this method, the stitching line is marked directly on the fabric. You sew right along the marked line, assured that the stitches are accurately placed. This approach is especially useful for small shapes that become difficult to maneuver under a moving sewing machine needle once they are cut out. By sewing before you cut, you reduce the chance of inaccuracy or accident. You'll also notice that these template patterns are marked "slit to turn." Instead of leaving an opening in the seam for turning, you will slit the sewn piece on the back to turn it right side out. Slitting the interior preserves the integrity of the shape outline.

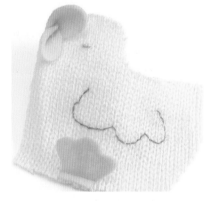

Cut First, Sew Later

A second, more traditional, pattern type does include seam allowances. These stitching lines are clearly marked with a broken line, usually ¼" (.5 cm) inside the cutting line. This construction method is used when sewing dissimilar pieces together or when special indicators are necessary.

Cutting Without a Pattern

A third method of patterning involves dimensional measurements. The instructions might read "cut a 10" x 12" (25 cm x 30 cm) rectangle" or "cut a 6" (15 cm) circle." For these types of shapes, accurate measuring and drafting are crucial.

Stuffing and Batting

Several of the sewing projects require stuffing or layering with quilt batting. Polyester fiberfill is recommended for stuffing. It remains fluffy and buoyant even after repeated washings. Use a point turner or the long handle of an artist's paintbrush to transport stuffing into hard-to-reach corners inside the project. For quilts or padded projects like the duck pond (page 63), use quilt batting. It comes in a variety of weights, thickness, and finishes. Use a batting appropriate for the project for optimum results.

Finishing Seams

Most baby sewing projects call for a ¼" or ½" (.5 cm or 1 cm) seam allowance. The project patterns and instructions will suggest the appropriate seam allowance. You can clean-finish the edges of woven fabrics by pinking with pinking shears, or by stitching close to the edge to prevent fraying. It is not necessary to finish the edges when sewing with knits or fleece fabrics.

Your Sewing Machine

If the promise of a new baby in the family has caused you to pull your sewing machine out of the back of a closet, do yourself a favor. Treat your machine to a servicing at your local machine dealer, or at the very least, do a thorough cleaning and oiling yourself. Most importantly, use a new needle. You'll be amazed at the improvement of your stitch quality.

Decorative Stitches and Hand Embellishment

Hand embroidery is a time-honored way to add details such as facial features. You might embellish a purchased fleece blanket with a contrasting blanket stitch or add a little flourish to a jacket or jumper. Handwork imparts a richness unlike any other medium, and it demonstrates a generous sharing of your time and effort to create a special gift for the new baby.

An added advantage is that hand stitching is perfectly safe for baby. You can use a simple running stitch or chain stitch for a whimsical smile, cross-stitch for the eyes, and several stitches close together for a nose. Here are four easy embroidery stitches that can be used for the projects in this book.

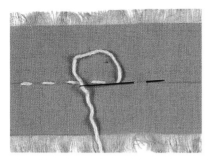

Running Stitch

The running stitch is a very basic stitch and involves no more than moving the needle in and out of the fabric at regular intervals.

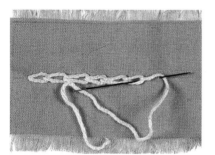

Chain Stitch

The chain stitch is one of the easiest decorative stitches to learn. It creates a heavier, fuller line that makes embroidered details more noticeable. Experiment with different weights and types of thread, yarn, and floss for a variety of results.

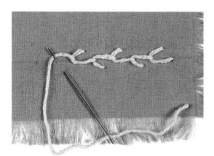

Feather Stitch

The feather stitch is based on the same premise as the chain stitch: the thread is caught and formed into shape with the needle. It would be perfect for creating a contrasting border on a baby quilt or blanket.

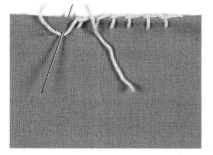

Buttonhole or Blanket Stitch

Used as a decorative edging on items such as blankets, cuffs, and collars, the buttonhole or blanket stitch handsomely accents the work while also providing a finished edge.

Image Transfer: Working with Inkjet-Printable Fabric

You are about to enter the twenty-first century of crafting. Using an ordinary home computer and color inkjet printer, you can now output and print any image you desire onto crafter-friendly printable fabric. The standard-size computer fabric sheets feature a paper carrier backing that facilitates movement through your printer. When the paper backing is removed, what remains is a tightly woven, fray-resistant cotton fabric, imprinted with your personally selected image and ready to be incorporated into a unique gift. The possibilities are endless!

Formatting

The first step is to select a format for your design using a computer graphics program. There are a number of simple, moderately priced graphics programs available, and they can be supplemented with purchased or on-line clip art collections. For projects where you want to print the full sheet, you would choose the blank "sign" or "poster" template. The soft picture book project (page 90) uses a quarter-fold greeting card template that lays out the book for you with the pictures oriented correctly. To make the eight-page book, simply design and print two "cards" instead of one.

Creating the Design

Creating your design is really a lot of fun. For the most part, the computer programs are simple, straightforward, and user-friendly. You will be able to write headlines and messages in a variety of type styles and colors. Some programs even offer a collection of ready-to-use poems and sentiments. You can add borders and clip art images from the program and lay them out any way you please.

Importing the Images

For the ultimate in personalization, family photographs and original children's art will make your projects truly one-of-a-kind. To get your own images into the computer, photograph them with a digital camera or scan them into the program. If you have neither a camera nor a scanner, many photo developers will burn your favorite photographs onto a disc or CD, making it very easy to transfer the images into your system. You can also work with images received via e-mail or through one of the photo web sites that lets you store images on-line.

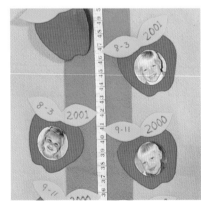

Fine-Tuning

Once the images are in the computer, use a photo-editing program to manipulate the image. Most of them guide you through the process step by step so that you can brighten or darken, play with colors and contrast, and size and crop them to your satisfaction. These programs are very easy to use while giving dramatic results. Get the whole family involved—you can bet that your kids will already know how to perform all these functions.

Printing

When you feel your design is complete, run a test print on a piece of paper. Sometimes colors or design elements look a little different on paper than they do on the screen. Adjust your image until you get it just the way you want it. Print the image on the fabric using an inkjet printer or copier. It is wise to put only one sheet of the fabric into the printer or copier at a time.

Using Your Printed Fabric

When your printed image is completely dry, remove the paper backing and rinse gently in cold water. This step removes any excess ink that might be sitting on the surface of the print. Do not wring out the fabric; instead, lay it flat on a smooth clean surface to dry. When it is dry, press out any wrinkles with an iron and then proceed to incorporate it into your project. If the need arises to launder the fabric, do not use detergent. Wash in cold water by hand or machine on a gentle cycle. If the fabric becomes soiled, use a cold water wash and add liquid fabric softener. Always lay the printed fabric flat to dry.

Congratulations! You are now on the cutting edge of fiber crafting.

Knitting Basics

There's something about the birth of a new baby that makes us want to reconnect to our family traditions. For many families, hand-knitted caps and booties represent as much of an expectant mother's tradition as, well, pickles and ice cream! If you've never knitted before, there's no better time to try your hand (literally) at this age-old craft.

The information collected here can help you get started or it might refresh your memory if it's been a while since you've picked up your knitting basket. The best way to learn is to get a friend or family member to spend an afternoon showing you the basics. Both the time that you share and the cuddly gifts that you knit will be treasured for many years to come

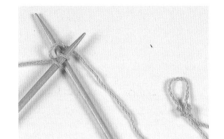

Step One

Near left: Make a noose by curving the end of the yarn back over itself. Pull the yarn through the resulting loop and tighten.

Far left: Slide the noose over the left knitting needle. Make a second noose and slip it onto the left needle. Slip the right needle between the nooses, starting at the bottom and ending behind the left needle. From the back side of the work, wrap the loose end of the yarn around the right needle, and pull it in between the two tools.

Step Two

Use the tip of the right needle to pull the yarn through the noose loop. There should be a new loop, or stitch, on the right needle. Transfer this stitch back to the left needle. Continue casting on until enough stitches have been formed for your project.

Step Three

Begin a knitting row by forming a stitch in the same manner as when casting on: Insert the right needle through the loop on the left needle, and pass the loose yarn between the two tools.

Step Four

Draw the yarn through to make a new stitch. This time, the new stitch will remain on the right needle, and the stitch from the previous row is dropped from the left needle.

Step Five

To work the stockinette stitch shown in these examples, the right-side rows are knitted and the wrong-side rows are purled. To purl, insert the right needle through a stitch on the left needle so that the right needle passes in front of the left needle. Pass the loose yarn around the right needle counterclockwise as shown.

Step Six

Pull the yarn through the stitch on the left needle, forming a new stitch on the right needle. Release the stitch from the left needle.

Step Seven

Casting off can be done on either a knit or a purl row. Begin by forming two stitches on the right needle as usual. With the left needle, pull the first stitch formed over the second and off the point of the right needle. There is now one stitch on right needle. Work the next stitch on the left needle so that there are two stitches on the right needle again.

Step Eight

Repeat the cast-off motion on the right needle. Continue until all stitches have been cast off. Clip the yarn and draw the tail through the one loop remaining.

Paper Crafting

Decorative papers can be used for announcements, covering albums and journals, for shower invitations, and in decoupage projects. By collecting different types of gift wrap, wallpaper borders, and specialty art papers, you'll always have a bountiful supply for spur-of-the-moment paper crafting.

Today's proliferation of cutting tools makes it easier than ever for even a beginner to achieve professional results. Paper punches, decorative-edge scissors, and circle and oval cutters produce clean-cut shapes and edges in a fraction of the time it would take to cut them by hand with scissors.

Here are some more paper embellishing techniques.

Scrape to Crayon

Scrape to crayon adds both funk and elegance to handcrafted wrapping papers, cards, and name tags, whether you choose bright colors with a controlled design or muted tones with wild, free-form gestures. Carving detail into a child's storybook or wall picture would add visual interest and transform the piece into a treasured heirloom.

Start by lightly penciling a design outline on white paper. Using wax crayons, fill the design area with different colors. Press hard so the colors are saturated. Brush black water-based paint over the entire surface, and let dry several hours. Then use a knitting needle or stylus to scrape off the black paint and reveal the multi-colored surface underneath. Be careful not to scrape too hard, or you will damage the crayon layer or the paper itself.

Paper Piercing

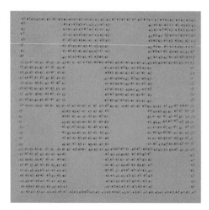

Piercing adds beautiful, delicate textures to paper. Try combining different sizes of needle holes to form a pattern. Piercing from both sides of the paper will also produce interesting texture variations. You can also use your sewing machine to do the piercing for you. Omit threading the needle and you can sew up a really fun design. Use preprogrammed stitches to create monograms and other piercing patterns.

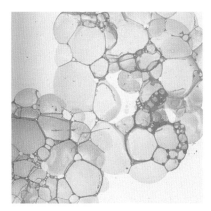

Bubble Marbling

The see-through quality of bubble marbling is fascinating and unexpected. The light and airy imprints are perfect additions to books, cards, and even children's wooden building blocks.

The technique couldn't be simpler. Mix liquid dishwashing detergent and water in roughly a four-to-one ratio. The consistency should resemble light cream. Select a paint color—use water-based acrylic paint or tempera thinned with water—and add it to the solution, stirring thoroughly to reach the desired intensity. Mix additional colors in separate bowls. Use a drinking straw to blow bubbles into the first color. Working a small area at a time, quickly lay a piece of paper facedown onto the bubbles, and then lift up. Set the paper aside for a moment or two to give any bubbles sitting on the surface a chance to pop. Then continue adding more colors in the same way.

Embossing

Embossing adds dimension and a sculptural quality to paper. Select papers that are supple enough to show embossed shapes clearly. You might even adapt one of the pattern templates such as our little bear head (page 122) to become an embossing template.

To make a pattern tile, cut the desired shapes out of chipboard and glue them to a chipboard backing that is slightly larger than the paper you want to emboss. Let dry. Lay the pattern tile design side up and cover with a sheet of plastic wrap to prevent sticking. Brush water on the paper and place it on top of the plastic wrap. Cover with a second sheet of plastic wrap, followed by several towels and a pressing board or large book. Stack additional heavy weights on top and leave overnight to dry. Use the finished piece to cover an album, as an accent for invitations, or to adorn a picture frame.

Baby's Room

During the long months of anticipation leading up to the arrival of a new baby, it's not uncommon for parents-to-be, often accompanied by family and friends, to focus their waking hours on "feathering the nest." For them, as for our feathered friends, only the finest available nesting materials will do. After all, the nursery presents an interesting dilemma. Since the room will most likely serve as the new baby's total environment for several months, the decor must be colorful and stimulating, yet at the same time provide a restful, calming respite from the busy universe beyond the door. Quite a tall order!

While Mom and Dad will probably want to make the major decisions, such as choosing the crib and color scheme, there are plenty of items that friends and family can provide to make the little one's paradise complete. Included in this chapter are four projects that make perfect gifts for a new nursery. All can be readily customized by color choice or fabric selection to suit just about any décor.

Little padded hangers are so cute, chances are they won't spend a lot of time hidden in a closet. Picture them hanging on pegs along the walls, or perhaps on a junior coat rack, displaying some of the adorable wee outfits that grandma can't resist shopping for every time she leaves the house.

The individual painted wooden alphabet letters offer a classic way to personalize the room while starting a budding genius on the road to becoming a man of letters.

And what better way than a computer to engage older siblings or cousins in a project for the baby's room? Our lampshade project lets them scan their original artwork and print it onto fusible fabric. They will love the results of their computer crafting and be delighted to be included in the proceedings.

Finally, our musical crib mobile with its simple patterns, high contrast, and constant movement will provide hours of stimulating entertainment for the little one during those first few precious months when he hasn't much else to do except, well, nap.

The Well-Dressed Closet

Decorative Padded Hangers

A GREAT IDEA FOR A REALLY CUTE SHOWER GIFT *is to make a set of decorative padded hangers, perfectly sized for baby's tiny wardrobe. Start with purchased children's hangers, or cut larger wooden hangers down to size. Pad each hanger with foam and batting, cover with colorful fabric, and embellish with a soft-sculpted flower to complete the look.*

Materials:

Wooden hanger

Two 8" x 8"(20 cm x 20 cm) pieces of cotton fabric

Two 4" x 8" (10 cm x 20 cm) pieces of fleece fabric

8" (20 cm) length of velvet tube ribbon

½" (1 cm) plastic button for center of flower

Matching sewing thread

12" x 1½"-diameter (30 cm x 4 cm-diameter) foam pipe insulation, or polyester batting

Polyester fiberfill

Sewing machine

Iron

Hand sewing needle

Pins

Point turner or artist's paintbrush

Air-soluble marking pen

Ruler

Scissors

Small handsaw (optional)

Flower and leaves templates (page 113)

Instructions

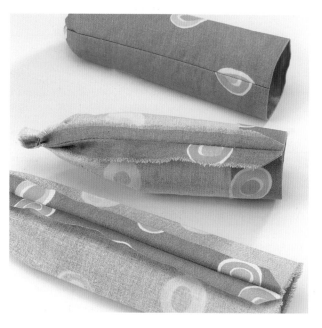

1. Saw off the ends of the wooden hanger so it measures about 11" (28 cm) across (or start with a children's hanger). Enclose the wooden portion of the hanger in foam pipe insulation, available at most home improvement stores, or if you prefer, wrap polyester batting around the hanger until the padding is 1" to 2 ½" (3 cm to 6 cm) in diameter.

2. Fold each 8" (20 cm) square of cotton fabric in half, right side in, and pin the edges together to make a tube. Test-fit each tube on the padded hanger arm (the fit should be fairly snug), and machine-stitch. Gather one end closed by hand-sewing a running stitch ½" (1 cm) in from the end and pulling tightly. To end off, wrap the thread several times around the gathered end, take a few stitches through all the layers, and knot securely. Press the open end of one tube ½" (1 cm) to the wrong side. Turn both pieces right side out. Insert polyester fiberfill or batting into each tube to plump out the gathered end.

A Word About

Ages and Stages

From the first hours of life, a newborn needs a stimulating environment to help her learn more about her own body and the world around her. With proper stimulation, learning can be greatly enhanced.

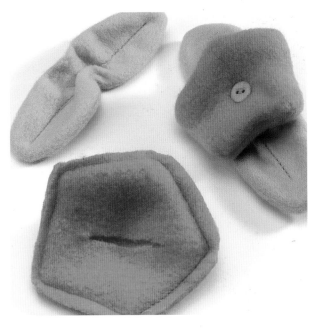

3. Remove the cording from the velvet tube ribbon, and thread the ribbon onto the metal portion of the hanger. Tuck in the ends and secure with a few hand stitches. (Note: If you prefer, you can create your own coordinating fabric sleeve from 1¼"-wide [3 cm-wide] bias tape or a bias-cut strip of fabric.) Place both fabric tubes on the padded hanger so they overlap at the center. Slip-stitch along the folded edge for an invisible finish.

Variation

For a more tailored version, create a cute teddy bear head as the embellishment. Use the small bear head template (page 122) and follow the instructions for making the head in the Wrist Rattle project (page 66).

4. Fold each 4" x 8" (10 cm x 20 cm) piece of fleece in half, right side in. Place the flower or leaves template (page 113) on the appropriate color fleece and trace the outline with an air-soluble pen. Do not cut out yet. Stitch on the marked lines all around through both layers. Cut out each piece ¼" (.5 cm) beyond the stitching line all around. Cut slits for turning in one layer only. Turn each piece right side out, using a point turner or the handle end of an artist's paintbrush to open out the shapes. Fold the leaves piece in half lengthwise, concealing the slit. Pinch together in the center to form two leaves and secure with a few stitches. Hand-sew the slit on the back of the flower. Sew the flower to the leaves, adding a bright button at the center, and then attach the entire piece to the hanger with a few stitches.

The ABCs of Decorating

Painted Wooden Letters

WITH THESE DECORATIVE WOODEN ALPHABET LETTERS, *it's as easy as ABC to create a charming nursery accent. Choose colors to coordinate with the room's decor or personalize the project further by spelling out the baby's name. Even a beginner can easily create the heart/leaf patterns shown here using a specially formulated "enamel" craft paint. The finished letters can be displayed on a shelf or dresser top or be adhered to the wall or a door.*

Materials:

5" (13 cm) wooden letters	Fine-grade sanding sponge
Décor-it! enamel-like paints: sea blue, lemon, apricot, kelly green, grass green, magenta	Tack cloth
	Stylus
1" foam brushes	

Instructions

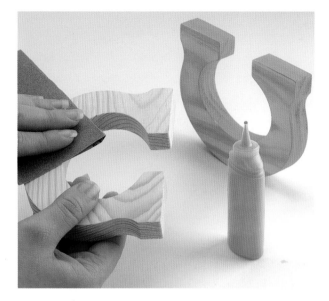

1. Sand each wooden letter with a fine-grade sanding sponge, and wipe clean with a tack cloth. Using a foam brush, paint the edges and back of each letter. Let dry, and then paint a second coat. Let dry overnight.

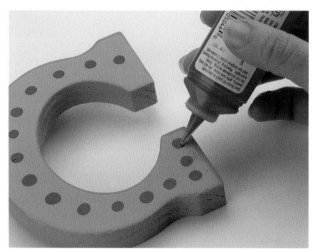

2. Choose two coordinating colors of Décor-it! paint. Using the applicator tip, flow the first color generously to the unpainted front surface of the wooden letter, making sure the coverage extends to the edges. While the first color is still very wet, apply dots of the second color along the center of the letter, spacing them about a dot's width apart.

A Word About
What Baby Sees

Adults tend to think of babies in terms of soft pastels, but the fact is that newborns, in particular, are most drawn to bold shapes in black, white, and red. If you really want to attract their attention, create some accents with strong contrasts in color and value. As the baby becomes more aware of her surroundings beyond the crib, she will appreciate the rich environment you provide.

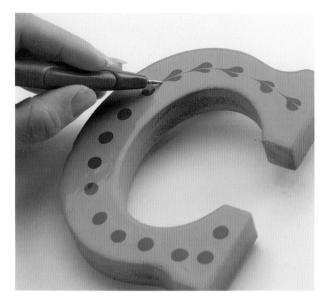

3. Beginning just beyond the edge of the first dot, drag the pointed edge of the stylus through the center of the dots. The special formulation of the paint will cause the colors to swirl, creating a leaf or heart design. Let dry completely. Use the same technique with different colors until you have decorated all of the letters.

Variation

Personalize any baby's room by using bright, bold primary colors to spell out the baby's name. Then use Décor-it! paint to embellish the letters with the design of your choice. The palette shown includes red, yellow, blue, white, and magenta. Have fun and be creative!

Just Kidding Around

Nursery Lamp Shade

EVEN UTILITARIAN ITEMS, *like this simple candlestick lamp, can add charm and interest to a baby's room. To make it easy, we used a self-adhesive shade that comes with its own pattern template. Self-adhesive shades are readily available at most craft stores, but you could also start with an inexpensive paper shade and simply cover it.*

The main design element in our shade is children's artwork, which we printed onto inkjet-printable fabric and fused to the shade cover. You could enlist one of baby's older siblings or perhaps a gaggle of young cousins to create the artwork for you—and to assist with the computer. And don't forget the trims—we finished the edges with giant chenille rickrack and added some shiny buttons just for fun. This colorful shade is sure to grab baby's attention whenever the lamp is switched on.

Materials:

4" x 11" x 7" (10 cm x 28 cm x 18 cm) self-adhesive lampshade

½ yard felt

1⅝ yards (1.5 meters) giant chenille rickrack

12 assorted plastic buttons

Three 8 ½" x 11" (22 cm x 28 cm) sheets of inkjet printable fabric

Three 8½" x 11" (22 cm x 28 cm) sheets of no-sew fusible adhesive

Extra-thick white craft glue

Iron and presscloth

Scissors, or rotary cutter and mat

Air-soluble marking pen

Spring-type clothespins

Instructions

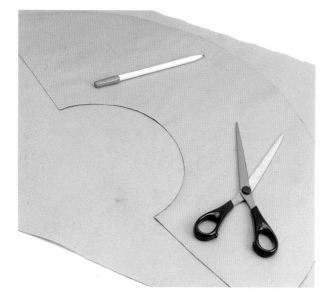

1. Remove the paper wrapper from the self-adhesive shade. Using the wrapper as a template, trace the shade shape onto felt with an air-soluble marker. Cut out the felt shade cover on the marked lines with a rotary cutter or scissors. (Note: If you are using woven fabric instead of felt, cut 1" (3 cm) beyond the marked lines all around.)

2. Scan, size, and print the selected artwork onto three printable fabric sheets (refer to pages 16–17). Apply fusible adhesive to the wrong side of each sheet, following the manufacturer's instructions. Cut out the images, arrange them on the felt shade cover, and fuse in place. Work from the center outward, letting some images overlap the edges as necessary.

A Word About
Design Sources

Instead of using children's artwork on a shade cover, substitute baby's photographs or some of the charming clip art images that are widely available in computer programs. You might also try a combination of the two.

3. Apply the felt shade cover to the shade, aligning the seam and top and bottom edges first. Work slowly and carefully, repositioning the cover as necessary to eliminate wrinkles. Press gently with your hand, smoothing from side to side and from top to bottom, until the cover adheres. Trim any excess fabric from the edges and seam. If the seam pops up, glue it down.

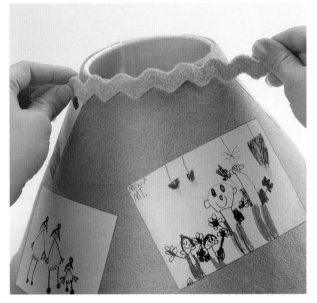

4. Starting at the seam and working a few inches at a time, apply a bead of glue around the upper edge of the shade. Glue on the rickrack so it extends slightly beyond the shade. Clamp with clothespins until dry. Trim the lower edge of the shade in the same way. Place the shade on the lamp base to avoid crushing the trim. Glue the buttons to the shade in a random arrangement.

Variation

Instead of using printable fabric art, trace some moon and star shapes onto felt. Apply fusible adhesive to the back of the felt, cut out the shapes, and fuse them to the shade cover in a random arrangement. The edging trim can be added or not, as desired.

Bold and Bright

Musical Crib Mobile

VISUAL STIMULATION *is of paramount importance to the newborn. Babies are naturally interested in their surroundings, and their primary interaction with their environment is visual. Recent studies show that this stimulus is the first step in preparing the brain for all learning that will follow. What better object to garner baby's attention than a bright, floating, ever-changing mobile above the crib?*

The simplest of craft materials are used for this mobile: the inner wooden ring from an embroidery hoop, chenille cord, plastic foam balls, plastic buttons, and trim. Each foam ball is covered with felt, which then becomes the foundation for color- ful rickrack, buttons, and additional felt shapes applied in bold, dazzling pat- terns. Baby will find this swirling mobile supremely eye-catching!

Materials:

Purchased crib mobile arm and musical turning mechanism

Inside ring from a 10" (25 cm) embroidery hoop

9" x 12" (23 cm x 30 cm) felt craft sheets: red, black, white, yellow

Chenille cord: 1⅔ yards (1.5 meters) each black and red

Scraps of giant chenille rickrack

Assorted plastic ½" to ¾" (1 cm to 2 cm) buttons

Four 4" (10 cm) plastic foam balls

1" (3 cm) metal jump ring (used for keys)

White acrylic craft paint

Extra-thick white craft glue

Brushes for paint and glue

Ball-head pins

Long soft-sculpture needle

Scissors

Instructions

1. Paint the embroidery hoop's inside ring white, and set it aside to dry. Meanwhile, wrap a sheet of felt snugly around each ball's equator, pinning as you go. When you reach the starting point, trim away the excess felt and butt the edges. Working in short intervals, unpin the felt, glue it to the ball, and then reinsert the pins. Continue the gluing and pinning process, gradually pulling the excess felt towards the two opposite poles of the ball.

2. When the felt begins bunching up near the poles, carefully trim away the excess and glue down the remainder flush against the ball's surface. Butt the cut edges for smooth, even coverage. Double-check to make sure the poles are directly opposite one another. Use pins to the hold the felt in place until the glue dries.

A Word About
Safety

Mobiles should be hung just out of reach of an infant. They should be removed from the crib when the baby begins to pull up—at about five months.

3. To decorate the balls, choose colors that create strong contrasts and vibrant patterns against the felt background. Cut and glue strips of chenille rickrack to two of the balls from pole to pole, covering the butted seams. Cut out and glue small felt circles or plastic buttons to the remaining two balls. Cut two circles, 3" (8 cm) or larger, and glue them over the poles to conceal the glued seams.

4. Hold the black and red chenille cords together, fold at the midpoint to make a loop, and hitch the loop to the metal jump ring. Hitch the four dangling cords at equidistant points to the painted ring so the ring is balanced and the ends of the cords hang freely. Thread a long soft-sculpture needle with one cord end. Insert the needle through a decorated ball from top to bottom, draw the cord through, and knot the end. Join the other three balls the same way. Attach the purchased mobile components to the crib, following the manufacturer's instructions, and hang the mobile.

Variation

Other plastic foam shapes such as cones, pyramids, and cubes can also be covered with felt and decorated. Keep the design simple, and feel free to experiment. Since baby is often gazing up at the mobile, try putting some friendly human faces or other highly contrasting patterns on the bottom of the shapes, where she can see them.

Baby's Clothes and Comforts

The arrival of a new baby always seems to trigger a flurry of personal appearances and photo opportunities worthy of a Hollywood celebrity. Family and friends all want to meet the new star in person, and those who live out of town anxiously await the latest round of photos. In order to meet the wardrobe demands of such a hectic schedule, the little star's clothing and accessories must be comfortable, colorful, and plentiful. Simple handmade gifts of clothing and soft, cozy baby blankets will be remembered long after they're outgrown, preserved forever in keepsake photos.

This section offers several projects that can be easily adapted to a variety of tastes and skill levels. The cute clothing ensembles are not hard to make. You can start with plain purchased one-piece underwear and add simple embellishments and accessories to personalize your gift. Only very basic sewing skills are required. There is even a variation that uses fusible adhesive so that nonsewers can get in on the act.

The playful activity blanket features fluffy fleece squares pieced together and embellished with a soft chenille rickrack trim. To add to the fun, loops sewn into the patchwork seams allow the attachment of small rattles and other interactive toys to engage and amuse the baby.

In a more traditional mode, an adorable little knitted cap, matching booties, and an easy-to-knit bib offer an excellent opportunity to learn a new skill or rekindle interest in an old one. However you choose to make baby comfortable and cozy, your gift is sure to be appreciated.

Pea-in-a-Pod

Cozy Baby Ensemble

THIS DELIGHTFUL PAIRING *of a color-coordinated receiving blanket and embellished one-piece knit underwear is the perfect outfit to keep a new baby warm and cozy as a pea in a pod. Wrapped in the soft flannel blanket, the baby will feel safe, snug, and secure.*

Basic sewing skills are all that are required. As a matter of fact, this project would make a good beginner's sewing project. Success and praise are guaranteed!

Materials:

One-piece snap-seat underwear	Iron
Two 1-yard (.9 meter) pieces of pre-washed cotton flannel in coordinating colors and patterns	Scissors
	Hand sewing needle
Matching sewing thread	Pins
Three green ½" (1 cm) flat buttons	Yardstick
	Air-soluble marking pen
Sewing machine	Peapod template (page 114)

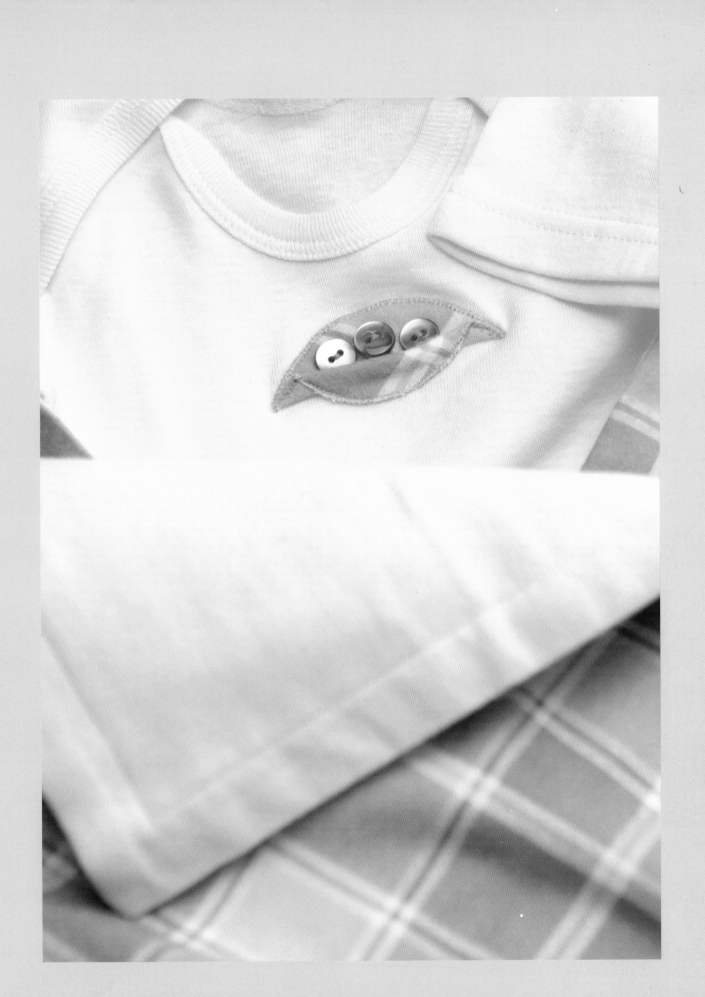

Instructions

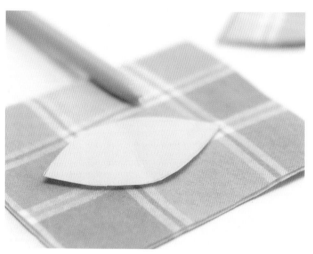

1. Mark and cut a 33" x 33" (84 cm x 84 cm) square from each piece of flannel. Layer the squares right sides together, and pin. Machine-stitch through both layers ½" (1 cm) from the edge all around, leaving an 8" (20 cm) opening along one edge for turning. Clip the corners, turn right side out, and press. Hand-sew the opening closed. Topstitch ¾" (2 cm) from the edge all around.

2. Fold a small piece of leftover flannel in half, wrong side in. Place the peapod template (page 114) on top; if using plaid fabric, place the template on the bias. Trace the outline with an air-soluble pen. Cut on the marked line through both layers. Sew a narrow zigzag stitch around the outside edges. Widen the zigzag slightly and sew around again.

A Word About

Buttons and Babies

Buttons have been used for generations as closures for babies' clothes and make great decorative accents. They must be carefully attached, however, to avoid a potential choking hazard. Use strong thread or dental floss to attach them through several layers of fabric. Check at every laundering to be sure that they've remained firmly attached.

3. Press the peapod flat, then fold it in half lengthwise and press a crease from point to point. Sew three green buttons in a row along one edge for the peas.

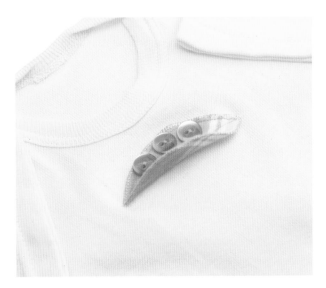

4. Center the peapod approximately 1" (3 cm) below the undershirt neckline, peas at the top. Using a zipper foot, sew the peapod to the shirt front along the center fold and upper curved edge; leave the lower half of the pod free. For added dimension, fold the lower half up at the sides and down at the middle, exposing the buttons. Press, then tack or topstitch to secure.

Variation

To coordinate baby clothing with a blanket, create a tiny pocket from the blanket fabric. Cut a 1½" x 3" (4 cm x 8 cm) rectangle of the blanket fabric. Fold it in half crosswise, right side out, and topstitch ¼" (.5 cm) from the fold for the pocket's top edge. Center the pocket 1" (3 cm) below the undershirt neckline and zigzag the side and bottom edges.

Patch and Play

Cuddly Activity Blanket

HERE IS A COLORFUL AND FUN PLACE *for baby to play that you can take with you wherever you go. This interactive play blanket features fluffy squares of soft fleece fabric with loops of chenille rickrack inserted in the seams to hold attachments for rattles, teething rings, and other essential toys. The attachments can be easily removed for washing when they're not helping those all-important toys stay put. The blanket's center block features a colorful appliqué made from a printed fabric.*

Materials:

Nine 12" x 12" (30 cm x 30 cm) squares of fleece fabric in assorted bright pastels

34" x 34" (86 cm x 86 cm) fleece fabric for backing

7" x 7" (18 cm x 18 cm) printed motif fabric in coordinating color

8½ yards (7.8 meters) giant chenille rickrack in assorted bright pastels (include 4 yards of one color)

7" x 7" (18 cm x 18 cm) light-weight fusible adhesive

Matching sewing thread

Four plastic attachment rings or hooks

Plastic rattles and teething rings with ring handles

Sewing machine

Iron

Scissors

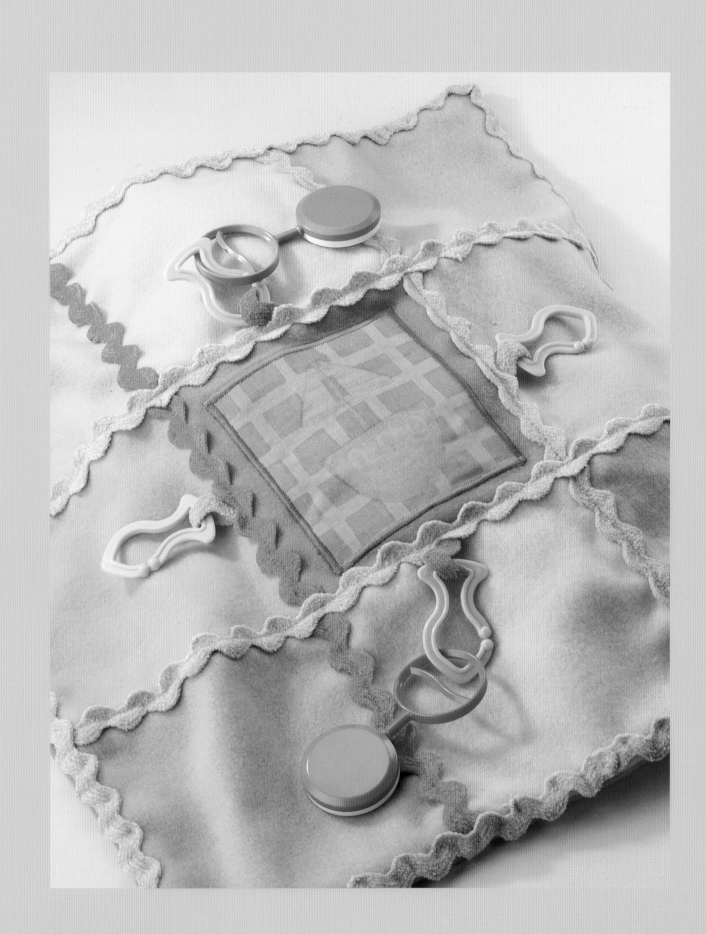

Instructions

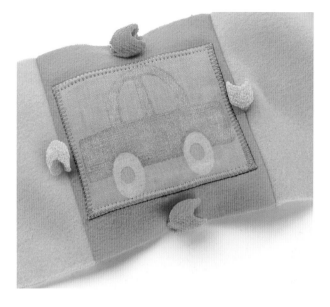

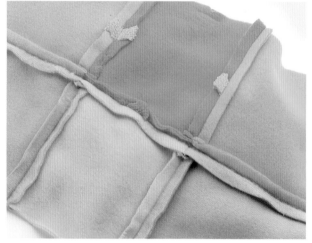

1. Apply the fusible adhesive to the wrong side of the printed motif square. Center the print on a fleece fabric square and fuse in place. Zigzag the appliquéd print around the edges. Cut four 4" (10 cm) pieces of rickrack. Fold each piece in half to make a loop. Stitch one loop to the middle of each edge of the fleece square. Sew coordinating fleece squares to the left and right edges with a ½" (1 cm) seam to make a three-patch strip.

2. Join the remaining six squares, making two rows of three squares each. Join the rows together so the appliquéd square is in the center and the seams match. Be sure the rickrack loops are firmly anchored in the seams.

A Word About

Baby's Fabrics

Choose soft natural fibers and easy-care blends for baby's clothing and bedding. Pay attention to the flammability labeling. Be sure to prewash all materials in gentle detergent before beginning your project to remove any scratchy sizing, insure colorfastness, and guard against fabric shrinkage.

3. Stitch the giant chenille rickrack over the seams, tic-tac-toe style. Make sure the loops are free and face out from the center block. Pin the blanket top to the backing, right sides together, and sew around the outside edge using a ½" (1 cm) seam allowance; leave an opening along one edge for turning. Turn right side out. Machine-stitch the opening closed. Pin and sew rickrack around the blanket's outside edge. Hand-tack in several places through all the layers to secure the front to the back. Attach the hooks and toys to the loops.

To vary the design, make a simple pocket on each patch. Cut a 5" x 6" (13 cm x 15 cm) fleece rectangle for each pocket. There is no need to hem fleece. Simply turn back the top edge 1" (3 cm) and topstitch for a mock cuff. Then pin the pocket to a fleece square and topstitch around the remaining three edges. It's easier if you sew the pockets in place first and then assemble the squares.

Daddy's Little Sweetheart

Appliqué Party Dress

IN THIS PROJECT, *you'll transform ordinary one-piece underwear into an adorable party dress worthy of "Daddy's Little Sweetheart." We used a raspberry-colored knit printed with tiny dots to make the heart appliqué and attached skirt. You'll probably want to make several of these in various fabric combinations, they are so quick and easy. Besides, a girl can never have too many party clothes!*

Materials:

One-piece snap-seat underwear	Sewing machine
⅓ yard (.3 meter) printed knit fabric	Iron
Small piece of lightweight fusible adhesive	Tape measure
	Scissors
Matching sewing thread	
	Air-soluble marking pen
Dental floss	
	Heart template (page 115)

Instructions

1. Following the manufacturer's instructions, apply lightweight fusible adhesive to a small piece of print fabric. Place the heart template (page 115) on the paper backing and trace around it with an air-soluble pen. Cut out the heart, and remove the paper backing. Center the heart on the underwear about 1" (3 cm) below the front neckline. Fuse in place. Zigzag around the edges to complete the appliqué.

2. For the skirt, cut a 10" x 45" (25 cm x 114 cm) strip of knit fabric. Zigzag over a length of dental floss on one long edge. Measure the underwear waist, and gather the floss edge of the skirt to match. For the waistband, cut a strip 1½" (4 cm) wide and 1" (3 cm) longer than the waist measurement. Sew the short ends of the waistband together using a ½" (1 cm) seam. If desired, clean-finish one edge of the waistband with a machine overcasting stitch.

A Word About

Comfort

Babies' skin is quite sensitive to fabric texture; they will appreciate your choosing soft knits and cottons for their wardrobes. Babies are also quite sensitive to any harsh dyes and chemicals that might be lurking. To ensure the utmost comfort, wash baby clothes and bedding separately from other family laundry in a very mild soap. Avoid heavily scented products such as laundry additives and bleaches.

3. Sew the short ends of the skirt together, clean-finish the lower edge, and sew a 1½" (4 cm) hem. Pin the raw waistband edge to the gathered skirt edge, right sides together; match the seams and distribute the gathers evenly. Stitch ½" (1 cm) from the edge all around. Trim the seam and press. Fold the waistband to the inside of the skirt, concealing the raw edges. From the right side, stitch along the seam line through all the layers. With the skirt seam at the center back, join the skirt to the underwear at the waist. Use a long zigzag stitch or stretch stitch, if available.

Variation

Other shapes look just as cute. Use a star template (page 115) or a teddy bear face template (page 122) to make a different appliqué. To eliminate the need for sewing, use a no-sew fusible adhesive.

Baby's First Outing

Knitted Cap and Booties

THIS LITTLE CAP AND BOOTIE SET *is best knit on a set of four straight double-pointed needles. Hold the work on three needles, and use the fourth needle as the worker. The knitting is worked in the round, always from the right side, so there are no seams to sew. If you like, change the yarn color on some of the rounds for a striped effect. Round ring markers slipped onto the needles will help you keep track of when to make the decreases. Make the cap for a newborn baby or knit the larger size for an older infant. The tiny booties will introduce you to the art of ribbed sock knitting. For a simpler project that's worked back and forth on straight needles, try the baby bib.*

Materials:

Cap and booties:

2 oz. (6 grams) washable wool fingering yarn

Set of four 6" size 3 double-pointed needles

Yarn or tapestry needle

Small ring markers

Gauge: 28 stitches = 4" [10 cm]

Sizes: Newborn (12 months)

Bib:

2 oz. cotton sport yarn

Size 5 straight needles

Yarn or tapestry needle

Gauge: 20 stitches = 4" [10 cm]

Size: Newborn

Instructions

Cap

For the cap, cast on 90 (120) stitches. Knit one row. Purl one row. Divide stitches evenly among three needles and work in the round as follows: Knit 1 round, purl 1 round, continue alternating in this way through round 10. Change to stockinette stitch (knit every round) and work until cap measures 3" (8 cm) (4" [10 cm]), or reaches the crown of the baby's head.

On the next round, ★ knit 13 (18) stitches, knit next 2 stitches together (one decrease), place a ring marker on the needle, repeat from ★ for 6 decreases evenly spaced all around. Continue knitting in the round, always working one decrease on the 2 stitches preceding each marker. Continue this pattern until 20 stitches remain. Break off the yarn about 20" (51 cm) from the top of the hat and thread the end through a yarn needle. Starting at the end of the row, run the needle through the remaining stitches, slip the stitches off the needles, and pull to gather. Weave the yarn end inside the hat for a few inches and end off.

A Word About
Keeping Your Baby Warm

Experts say that with proper clothing, babies can go out in just about any weather. Protect your baby from the elements by taking along several extra layers of clothing or blankets to accommodate changes in temperature during an outing. Our knitted cap and booties provide the perfect solution to keeping those little extremities warm and toasty. Be sure to remove them once you're inside since babies generate their own heat, just as you do.

Booties

For each bootie, cast on 36 stitches. Divide stitches evenly among three needles and work in the round as follows: ★ Knit 1, purl 1, repeat from ★ all around. Continue this pattern until bootie measures 3½" (9 cm) from the start. On the next round, ★ knit 10 stitches, knit next 2 stitches together (one decrease), place a ring marker on the needle, repeat from ★ for 3 decreases evenly spaced all around. Knit one round (33 stitches) without decreasing. Knit one round, working one decrease on the 2 stitches preceding each marker. Knit one round (30 stitches) without decreasing. Knit remaining rounds as decrease rounds until 9 stitches remain. Break off the yarn about 10" (25 cm) from the bootie toe. End off as for the cap. For each bootie tie (make two), cast on 2 stitches. Knit 1 row, purl 1 row, continue until tie is 10" (25 cm) long. Cast off. Using needle and yarn, tack midpoint of tie to bootie 1" (3 cm) below top edge. Place the bootie on the baby's foot so the strands wrap around the ankle and tie in front.

Bib

For the bib, cast on 35 stitches. ★ Knit 1, purl 1, continue across row, end knit 1. Repeat from ★ to make moss stitch pattern until work measures 3" (8 cm) from beginning. On the next row, slip 1 stitch to the right needle as if to knit, knit 1, pass the slipped stitch over knitted stitch and off the needle (left-facing decrease), ★ purl 1, knit 1 (break the moss stitch pattern), repeat from ★ to last 2 stitches, knit last 2 stitches together (right-facing decrease). Next row: Work moss stitch pattern. Next row: Work decrease on 2 stitches, work moss stitch, work decrease on last 2 stitches. Work last two rows again. Next row: Work moss stitch pattern. Next row: Work decrease on 2 stitches, ★ purl 1, knit 1 across row (break the moss stitch pattern), work decrease on last 2 stitches. Work 8 more rows in moss stitch, decreasing at beginning and end of every other row until 19 stitches remain. Cast off. For each bib tie (make two), cast on 3 stitches. Knit 1 row, purl 1 row, continue until tie is 9" (23 cm) long. Cast off. Using needle and yarn, tack the ties to the bib cast-off row.

Baby's Toys

Nothing is quite as satisfying as watching a baby engage with a toy that you've made yourself. There is something intrinsically delightful in observing this tiny creature exploring a new toy through all of his newly awakened senses—sight, sound, touch, hearing, and even taste.

Scientific research of recent years tells us much about how babies learn and how we can help them to reach their maximum potential. By observing how babies react to various stimuli at different ages, we can enrich each stage of development by offering toys appropriate to it.

The toys in this section are designed to provide a baby with a variety of visual, tactile, and auditory stimuli. As with all the projects in this book, you can customize the colors and fabrics to suit your own preferences.

Our squishy little sweater ducks and their colorful pond offer baby a wonderful visual and tactile treat while simultaneously providing all his adoring relatives with a delightful waterfront location for photo opportunities.

The little wrist rattle and rattle socks can help baby learn about the connection between cause and effect. She moves her hands or kicks her feet and something wonderful happens! A fun noise! When attached to her arms and legs, the rattles fall just within baby's focus. Best of all, she can't toss them away like traditional rattles, so they make life a littler easier for the new mother.

Our soft blocks invite all manner of creative play and will come in really handy when the baby starts to experiment with projectile physics, i.e., throwing stuff for the sheer joy of it! The blocks are colorful, soft, safe, and washable, all supreme qualities for a toy to possess.

The adorable denim teddy is sure to become a favorite friend. His plump little arms and legs are perfect for grasping by tiny hands, and the charming little details such as the pocket and hand-stitched face recall that simpler time in our own lives when playing with toys was our most important job.

Fine Feathered Friends

Sweater Duck Family

BABY'S FIRST BIG TRIP *may very well be to the home of his new best friends, the sweater ducks. Their plush pond is located conveniently on the floor of the nursery, so travel time is short and visits can be frequent. As their name would imply, the ducks are made of recycled sweater fabric that has been fortified with fusible tricot lining. Eye and wing details come alive with simple embroidery, and feet and bills are cut from felt. The pond is big enough for baby and several of his new quackers. It includes extra-soft hook-and-loop fastener tabs around the edges. Pinch the tabs and secure with florets to create a gently raised rim, much like the shape of a lily pad. It's a field trip baby will enjoy time and time again.*

Materials (for three ducks):

Yellow knit sweater (or ½ yard knit fleece [.5 meter] or velour fabric)

Bright yellow felt

Matching sewing thread

Blue and brown yarn

1 yard ¼"-wide (.5 cm-wide) green ribbon (optional)

½ yard fusible tricot stabilizer

Polyester fiberfill

Sewing machine

Iron

Scissors

Tapestry needle

Air-soluble marking pen

Duck templates (pages 116–117)

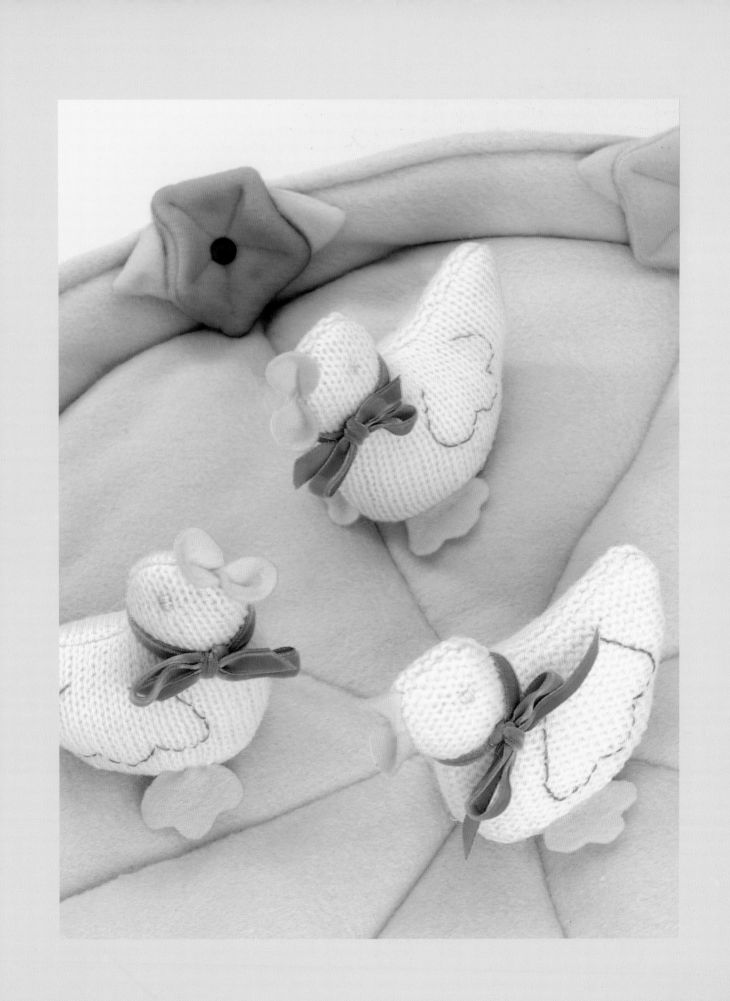

Instructions

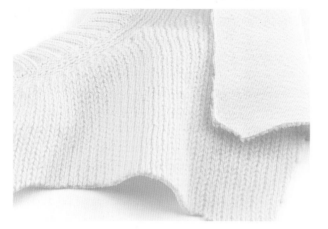

1. Prewash and dry the sweater. Cut open the seams and separate the sweater into sections that can be laid flat. Apply the fusible tricot to the wrong side of sweater fabric, following the manufacturer's instructions.

2. Use the sweater duck templates (pages 116–117) and an air-soluble marker to mark two duck bodies and one duck bottom on the sweater fabric. Also mark one duck bill and two duck feet on yellow felt. Cut out all the pieces. Repeat for each duck desired.

3. Using yarn and a tapestry needle, embroider a blue eye and a brown wing outline on each duck body. Fold the felt bill in half lengthwise and then crosswise, pinching and overlapping as shown in the diagram (page 117) for a three-dimensional effect. Pin the bill to one duck body and anchor it by machine-stitching along the seam line. Machine-stitch one felt foot to each body.

Plush Pond

4. Pin two duck bodies together, right sides facing, and sew using a ¼" (.5 cm) seam allowance; leave the bottom edge open. Pin the duck bottom to the body, right sides together, and stitch around, leaving a small opening in one side for turning.

5. **Inset:** Turn the duck right side out and stuff with polyester fiberfill. Hand-sew the opening closed. Tie a 10" (25 cm) length of ribbon around each duck's neck, if desired. Tack the ribbon securely to the duck with a few stitches so baby can't pull it off.

To make the pond, cut two 36" (91 cm) fleece circles (make one blue) and one 36" (91 cm) batting circle. Pin the pieces together, batting on the outside, and sew all around, leaving an opening for turning. Turn right side out so the batting is sandwiched in between, and hand-sew the opening closed. Topstitch ½" (1 cm) from the edge and again 1½" (4 cm) from the edge all around to define the lip of the pond. Use a yardstick and an air-soluble marker to draw four lines dividing the pond into eight equal pie-shaped sections. Topstitch on the marked lines. Cut eight 2¼" (5 cm) lengths of hook-and-loop fastener, and separate the pieces. Sew the loop pieces to the pond rim, straddling the topstitched spokes. Make eight fleece flowers (see pages 27 and 117); sew the hook pieces to the leaf undersides. To highlight the pond lip, pinch the rim at each spoke and press a flower against it to hold the pinch in place.

A Word About

Safety

To prevent a choking hazard, use either dental floss or very strong upholstery thread to sew the buttons onto the pond flowers. An alternative to buttons would be to embroider the flower centers or appliqué a small piece of green fleece at the flower center.

Shake, Rattle, and Smile

Teddy Bear Wrist Rattle

HERE IS A TOY *designed to stimulate and enhance a baby's sensory experience in a variety of ways as she develops from month to month. Attaching the rattle to baby's wrist allows her to get a good look at it, since her focus is clearest about seven to eight inches from her eyes. At two to three months, she will attempt to reach out and bring stimulating objects closer. As the baby flails and stretches, the rattle sounds reinforce and encourage movement and hand-eye coordination. Once she becomes more able to grasp at things, she will enjoy the soft squishy feel and texture of fabrics. The project is fairly simple, with just basic sewing and embroidery required.*

Materials:

4" x 8" (10 cm x 20 cm) gold fleece fabric

2" x 8" (5 cm x 20 cm) pink fleece fabric

Matching sewing thread

Black and red embroidery floss

1" (3 cm) length of soft hook-and-loop fastener

Small plastic rattle insert

3½" x 5" (9 cm x 13 cm) muslin

Polyester fiberfill

Sewing machine

Embroidery needle

Hand sewing needle

Pins

Point turner or artist's paintbrush

Scissors

Air-soluble marking pen

Bear head template (page 122)

Instructions

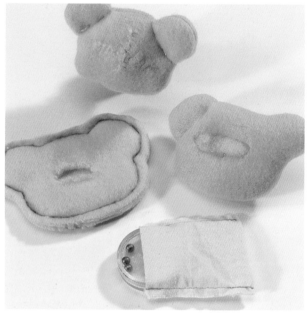

1. Fold the 4" x 8" (10 cm x 20 cm) gold fleece fabric in half, right side in. Place the bear head template (page 122) on top and trace the outline with an air-soluble pen. Do not cut out yet. Stitch on the marked line all around through both layers. Cut out the head ¼" (.5 cm) beyond the stitching line all around. Clip the curved seams around the ears as necessary.

2. Cut the slit for turning in one layer only. Turn the head right side out, using a point turner or the handle end of an artist's paintbrush to open out the shape. Topstitch to define the ears. Sew a small muslin sack, insert the rattle, and stitch closed. Poke some fiberfill into the bear head to round out the edges, insert the rattle, and then add more stuffing around the rattle until the head is plump and full. Hand-sew the slit closed.

A Word About

Plastic Rattles

When making baby rattles, always enclose the plastic shaker in a muslin sack and stitch it closed. That way, if the plastic housing is somehow broken, no tiny parts can escape.

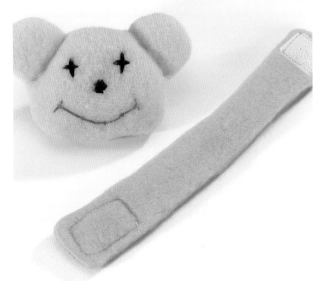

3. To make the strap, fold the 2" x 8" (5 cm x 20 cm) pink fleece in half lengthwise, and stitch across one end and down the long cut side. Turn right side out, tuck in the raw edges, and topstitch closed. Machine-stitch the hook and loop fastener halves to opposite ends of the strap for an overlapping closure. Mark the bear's facial features with an air-soluble pen and hand-embroider them with black and red thread. Tack the finished head securely to the middle of the strap.

As a variation, make two rattle bear heads. Attach them to a pair of socks so baby can amuse herself whenever she kicks up her heels!

Soft and Squishy

Stuffed Fabric Blocks

FIRST TOYS *are truly the building blocks of a child's imagination. In the first year, babies learn to experience their environment through all their senses, so it's important to provide them with stimulating shapes, colors, and textures.*

Crafted from colorful cotton fabric squares, these soft blocks make a playful addition to a baby's toy collection. They are easy and fun to make, whether you use new prewashed fabrics or scraps left over from other sewing projects. Fill the blocks with fluffy polyester fiberfill or precut foam blocks so that tiny hands can easily grasp the squishy surface. Cloth blocks travel well and can be tossed in the wash as necessary.

Materials:

Assorted cotton fabrics

Matching sewing thread

Polyester fiberfill, or 4" (10 cm) foam blocks

Sewing machine

Hand sewing needle

Pins

Scissors

Ruler

Air-soluble marking pen

Instructions

1. For each block, mark and cut six 5" (13 cm) squares of cotton fabric. Be sure to cut on the straight grain of the fabric to prevent puckering. Vary the pattern, texture, and color of the fabric squares for each block. Plan to place contrasting patterns next to one another and repeats opposite one another.

2. Machine-stitch four squares together end to end, with the right sides facing, using a ½" (1 cm) seam allowance. Join the two ends together to make an open box.

A Word About
Ages and Stages

At about six months, your baby will begin to understand the relationship between her actions and the results of them. She will continually experiment with cause and effect by throwing or dropping a toy. Soft blocks are the perfect laboratory equipment for your little physicist's experiments.

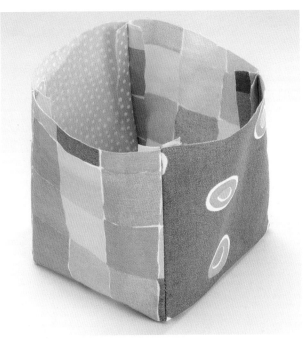

3. Pin the fifth square to one open end, right sides together and corners matching. Sew all the way around. Repeat at other end with the sixth square, but leave one side open for turning.

4. Trim the seam allowances and corners, turn right side out, and stuff with polyester fiberfill. If using foam blocks, compress a block to insert it into the opening. Slip-stitch the opening closed for a nearly invisible finish.

Variation

For a variation, make the blocks from fuzzy-textured fleece fabrics or soft terry towels.

My Favorite Teddy

Denim Teddy Bear

JUST ABOUT EVERY BABY *has a favorite toy that becomes legendary—literally, he can't leave home without it! This cute little denim teddy is a strong contender for that title. He's the perfect size, his little arms and legs are just right for grasping, and his face is always smiling. Constructed of sturdy denim, he is completely machine-washable and can stand up to lots of abuse (and love!). But most of all, he's just plain charming. Make him out of recycled denim for the softest teddy around. If starting anew, prewash the denim several times with fabric softener so the bear will feel like an old friend from the very first hug.*

Materials:

⅓ yard (.3 meter) soft denim or chambray

3" x 3" (8 cm x 8 cm) contrasting denim for pocket

3" x 3" (8 cm x 8 cm) colorful fabric for hanky

Matching sewing thread

Black and red embroidery floss

Polyester fiberfill

Sewing machine

Iron

Point turner or artist's paintbrush

Embroidery needle

Air-soluble marking pen

Teddy head, body, pocket, and hanky templates (pages 120–121)

Instructions

1. Fold the denim in half, right side in. Place the teddy body template (page 120) on top, and trace the outline with an air-soluble pen. Cut on the marked line through both layers. Mark and cut one pocket (page 121) from contrasting denim and one hanky (page 121) from a colorful fabric. Fold and press the pocket edges ¼" (.5 cm) to the wrong side. Fold the hanky and sew it to the back of the pocket. Topstitch the pocket to one bear body. Add a second row of topstitching for a jeans look.

2. Pin the two bodies right sides together. Stitch all around, leaving the neck open. Cut a 5" x 10" (13 cm x 25 cm) piece of matching denim. Fold it in half, right side in. Place the teddy head template (page 121) on top, and trace with an air-soluble pen. Do not cut out yet. Instead, machine-stitch on the marked line all around. Cut ¼" (.5 cm) beyond the stitching line all around. Cut a slit for turning in one layer only. Clip all the curves and inside points. Turn the head and the body pieces right side out.

A Word About
Washing Stuffed Toys

Place stuffed toys in a mesh bag and machine-wash on a gentle cycle. Tumble-dry on the no-heat setting, or simply let the toy air-dry.

3. Topstitch the head to define the ears. Stuff fiberfill into the head; sew the opening closed, turning in the slit's raw edges slightly. Mark and embroider the bear's eyes, nose, and mouth. Stuff fiberfill into the body, poking it down into arms and legs. Topstitch to define the arm joints and shoulders. Make sure there is no fiberfill in the neck. To clean-finish the neck, press the raw edge ¼" (.5 cm) to the inside and sew closed.

4. To join the head and body, pin the neck to the back of the head, concealing the slit. Carefully handstitch all the way around, even under the chin, to make a flexible, movable neck joint.

Variation

For a girl teddy, omit the pocket and make a little skirt out of fleece or another soft knit fabric. Follow the instructions for the appliqué dress (page 52). Make a hair bow from the hanky pattern. Fold the fabric in half, and stitch around the raw edges. Cut a slit in the middle of one layer only, and turn right side out. Pinch the middle, secure with a few stitches, and plump out the bow. Tack the bow to the top of the bear's head between ears. To prevent a choking hazard, use dental floss or upholstery thread instead of ordinary sewing thread.

Baby's Memories

The projects in this section all revolve around that all-important obsession, preserving and displaying a pictorial history of the baby from Day One. After waiting nine long months for the baby to arrive, the new parents just can't wait to get those first pictures framed, into the album, in the mail, or up on the Web.

The birth announcement is another vital item in baby's growing dossier. When it's time to tell the world that your little prince or princess has finally arrived, what better way to do it than with a clever announcement designed especially with your baby in mind.

If there is one aspect new parents notice right away, it's that a new baby changes literally every day. It's important to keep a camera on hand and take the time to snap a few shots chronicling each unfolding miracle. To organize the family's photographic journey, use an album featuring a handmade cover. Start with any standard purchased album that meets your preferred photo dimensions. We suggest using loose-leaf-style binders so that more pages can be added as soon as those darling photos come in.

In addition to giving you ideas for preserving and displaying photos and other mementos, the projects here also offer a rich selection of craft media to explore. Whatever your crafting interests—working with polymer clay, paper crafting, sewing, even computer image transfer—there's bound to be a project or two here that you'll be eager to try. So jump right in and try something new. You'll make a great gift for baby while learning a new skill.

Bears and Blocks

Clay-and-Wire Photo Holder

SHOW OFF THE LATEST PHOTOS *of the new baby with this whimsical wire photo clip. A polymer clay bear perched on a colorful clay-covered block holds the coil aloft. Photos can be easily removed for passing on to a friend or relative or for placement in an album when the next batch arrives.*

This is a great introductory project to working with polymer clay. We used an inexpensive push mold to make the bear and simply rolled out sheets of clay to cover a purchased wooden block. Best of all, the clay can be cured right in your home oven. Shiny craft beads add a bright embellishment to the wire clip.

Materials:

Soft polymer clay, 2 oz. (6 grams) each: caramel brown, blue, pink, yellow

2¼" teddy bear plastic push mold

1½" (4 cm) unfinished wood block

Craft armature wire

Multicolored craft beads, to fit wire

Extra-thick white craft glue

Polymer clay slicing blade

Craft knife

Needle-nose pliers

Wire cutters

Thick dowel or clay roller

Sheet of cardboard

Toothpick or embossing tool

Brush for glue

Drill and drill bit to match wire

Parchment paper or aluminum foil

Cookie sheet

Instructions

1. Knead the caramel-colored clay until soft. Press the clay into the teddy bear mold. Unmold the bear, place it on a hard work surface, and trim away the excess clay. Etch in the ears, mouth, and paws with a toothpick. Knead a bit of yellow clay, roll it flat, and cut out a bow tie shape. Roll a thin rope of yellow clay, wrap it around the bear's neck, and press the bow tie into place. Insert armature wire through the bear's arm to make a channel for the wire clip. Reshape the bear so it's sitting upright.

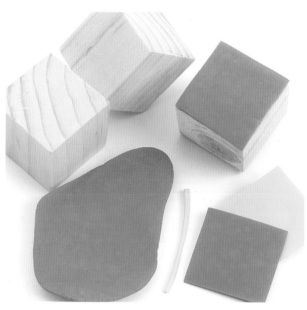

2. Knead the blue, yellow, and pink clays until soft. Roll each piece flat, wiping the dowel clean between colors. Set the 1½" (4 cm) wooden block on the yellow clay and cut around it with the craft knife. Repeat to cut two blue squares and two pink squares. Brush a small amount of glue on the block and affix the five clay squares to it, yellow square on top. Roll thin ropes of yellow clay, shape them into letters, and affix them to the blue and pink squares. Preheat the oven to 265°F (use an oven thermometer to verify the temperature). Place the bear and the block on a parchment- or foil-lined cookie sheet. Bake 20 to 30 minutes. Let the clay cool in the oven before removing it.

A Word About
Working with Polymer Clay

Polymer clay artists employ all kinds of kitchen utensils to create their magic. You can use a food processor to make the clay soft or to mix up a batch of a special color, small cookie cutters to create shapes, a garlic press to make hair, a rolling pin for creating slabs, and a cheese slicer for cutting thin strips. Just be sure that you keep your clay tools separate from those you actually cook with. Finish up by baking the final project in your home oven! Mmmm, what fun!

3. Cut an 11" (28 cm) length of craft armature wire. Using needle-nose pliers, curve one end of the wire back on itself to create a spiral with several concentric loops and a tail about 6" (15 cm) long. Attach two small brightly colored beads by bending the inside tip of the spiral and securing the beads with a drop of glue. Let dry.

Variation

For an alternative to the polymer clay base, try purchased baby's blocks to display those treasured photos. Use two blocks on the bottom and place the third block on top. Play with the blocks a little, staggering them and turning them so different sides are exposed until you find a composition you like. Then glue them together. Instead of one wire holder, make two. Drill two holes in the top block and glue in the wires. It's quick, easy, and fun to do!

4. Using a small brush, highlight the inside of the bear's ears and feet with light tan paint. Paint a small white circle for each eye, let dry, and then add a dot of black paint for the pupil. Paint the nose black, and add black freckles. Let dry completely. Sit the bear on top of the block, insert the wire coil, and mark its position. Drill a hole in the block at this spot to extend the channel. Test-fit all the pieces, trimming the wire as needed until the spiral is at a comfortable height. Place a small amount of glue in the block hole and on the bottom of the bear, glue the pieces together, and hold in place until the glue begins to set. Let dry overnight.

Baby's First Year

Photo Memory Album

THE WHIMSICAL WRAPAROUND DESIGN *on our album cover started out as a wallpaper border. Make a quick trip to any major home improvement outlet and you'll find a number of nursery wall borders that are the perfect size for embellishing an album. Our sample piece is a die-cut design; for a coordinated look, try a piece left over from decorating baby's room. The other specialty item you'll need is handmade paper. It comes in a wide variety of colors, textures, and styles and is available at most art supply stores. Or you might try creating your own decorative papers using the techniques on pages 20 – 21. This is such an easy cut-and-glue project, you'll want to make several. For a different effect, try the project variation. Most proud parents need more than one volume to do justice to the most beautiful baby in the world.*

Materials:

8" x 8½" (20 cm x 27 cm)
photo album

22" x 30" (56 cm x 76 cm)
textured paper

24" (61 cm) length of wall border

Extra-thick white craft glue

1" (3 cm) foam brush

Scissors

Ruler

Instructions

1. Open the album and lay it flat on the textured paper. Cut 1½" (4 cm) beyond the edge of the album all around. Fold the paper margins to the inside of the album, creasing the edges to measure for a snug fit. Remove the album from the paper. Apply a bead of glue around the edges of the album's spine and smooth the textured paper into position. In the same way, glue the paper to the album front cover and back cover. Work with the album in the closed position to ensure that the textured paper doesn't bind or restrict the album's opening and closing.

2. Apply a bead of glue on one inside edge of the album. Spread the glue evenly with a 1" (3 cm) foam brush. Gently fold the paper over, pressing it into place. Fold and glue the opposite edge in the same way. Trim diagonally at the corners and cut away the excess paper to reduce bulk. Glue down the remaining two sides. Let dry for at least one hour.

A Word About
A Sticky Situation

Choose a glue that is capable of adhering diverse surfaces such as plastic to paper, metal to fabric, and the like. A good thick white glue that becomes tacky immediately and dries clear will make your projects go smoothly and will ensure the professional results you desire.

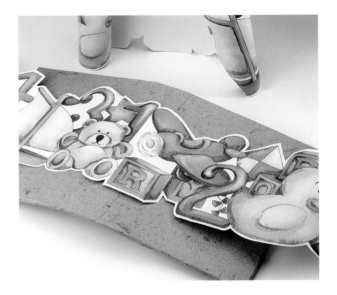

3. Open the album and lay it cover side up. Lay the wall border across it, adjusting its position so that an appropriate design falls on the front cover. Cut the wall border 1½" (4 cm) beyond the album edges at each end. Brush glue evenly on the wrong side of the wall border. Smooth the border into place around the album cover and onto the inside edges. As in step 1, work with the album in a closed position.

4. Measure the inside front and back covers. Cut a piece of textured paper for each. Trim the three outside edges by about ¼" (.5 cm). Test-fit each piece, and retrim if necessary. Using a foam brush, apply glue to the underside of the paper and spread it evenly. Press the papers into position. Let dry.

Variation

For a fabric-covered album, pad the cover first by gluing on several layers of plump quilt batting. The overall procedure is the same as for a paper cover. The key is to plan where the printed design will fall and to cut the fabric on-grain. If a fabric is loosely woven or tends to fray, a fusible tricot backing will stabilize it while maintaining flexibility. The ribbon ties are glued to the inside covers before the protective paper covering is added.

Spreading the News

Keepsake Birth Announcements

INSTEAD OF ORDERING *preprinted birth announcements, make your own using today's newest paper crafting techniques. The need for multiple cards gives you the perfect excuse to gather friends around the table for a fun-filled afternoon of cutting and pasting, perhaps in conjunction with the baby shower. The cards can all be prepared in advance, ready for the new mom to fill in the pertinent information once the baby arrives. Here are five innovative birth announcements to inspire you.*

Materials:

"Bonjour!" Card:

7" x 10" (18 cm x 25 cm) blue card stock

Card stock scraps: pink, white, green with white dots, peach, yellow, turquoise, lime green, black

4" x 4" (10 cm x 10 cm) white vellum

Punches: Super jumbo 1⅞" (5 cm) circle, super jumbo 1⅞" (5 cm) cartoon, super giant 2¼" (6 cm) oval, small 1" (3 cm) oval, small 1" (3 cm) teardrop, medium ⅝" (1.5 cm) circle, water splat

Ribbon punches: ¼" (5 mm) circle, ⅛" (3 mm) circle, dot

Decorative-edge scissors: scallop, deep zigzag

Extra-thick white craft glue

Black fine-point marker

Ribbon-Tied Bib Card:

5" x 7" (13 cm x 18 cm) medium yellow card stock

5" x 7" (13 cm x 18 cm) mint green vellum

6" x 8" (15 cm x 20 cm) white marble vellum

½ yard (.5 meter) pale yellow ³⁄₁₆"-wide (.25 cm-wide) picot-edged ribbon

4" x 6" (10 cm x 15 cm) double-sided adhesive

White gel pen

Computer with inkjet printer, or calligraphy pen

Decorative-edge "cloud" scissors

Super jumbo 1⅞" (5 cm) circle punch

Ribbon punches: teardrop, ¼" (5 mm) hole, ⅛" (3 mm) hole, dot

Scissors

Pencil

Bib and ruffle templates (page 118)

Patchwork Quilt Card:

Purchased blank 4" x 5" (10 cm x 13 cm) card and envelope

Contrasting card stock

Black fine-tip marking pen

Extra-thick white craft glue

Scissors

Ruler

Pencil

Snuggie Baby T-shirt Card:

White or pastel card stock

Purchased envelope

Black fine-tip marking pen

Scissors

Pencil

Baby T-shirt template (page 119)

Ansley Elizabeth

9*6*2001

7:53 p.m.

Instructions

"Bonjour!" Card

Use various punches and scissors to cut the shapes for this card, adding or omitting detail as desired. Start by punching a peach super jumbo circle "bib" and gluing it to white vellum. Trim the vellum with the deep zigzag scissors and punch ⅛" (3 mm) holes and dots to make a lace ruffle. Glue the bib at an angle to the card front. Glue on a large pink super jumbo circle "face" to overlap the bib. Add yellow water splat "hair" and ¼" (.5 cm) pink circle "ears." Draw in a mouth and nose with a black fine-tip marker. Glue on green super giant oval shoes; cut a white super giant oval in half to make the heels. Glue on medium pink circles for hands. Assemble a rattle from a narrow strip of yellow card stock and a medium yellow circle accented with a scalloped turquoise strip. To make the ring at the end of the handle grip, punch a ⅛" (.25 cm) hole in the yellow paper, then punch a ¼" (.5 cm) circle around it. For the baby bottle, cut a small white oval at an angle, glue it to the back of a small vellum oval, and top with a small peach teardrop "nipple" and a white bottle cap. Make the bib's car appliqué with a medium green half-circle, two small black circle "tires," and two quarter-circle "windows." Print the greeting of your choice on white paper and use the cartoon punch to cut around it.

Ribbon-Tied Bib Card

Using the bib and ruffle templates (page 118), trace one bib on the mint green vellum, one ruffle on the white marble vellum, and one narrow oval ring on the double-sided adhesive. Cut out all three pieces. Punch a super jumbo circle in the green bib for the neck opening. Scallop the ruffle's outer edge with the "cloud" scissors. Apply the self-adhesive ring to the back of the bib and affix the ruffle. To simulate white eyelet, draw white lines on the ruffle and punch teardrops, ⅛" (.25 cm) holes, and dots, as shown in the diagram (page 118). Place the bib on the yellow card stock. Plan the baby's name, birthdate, and any other details you want to share, to show through the green vellum bib; print the lettering by computer or by hand with a calligraphy pen. To attach the bib, position it on the yellow card, punch two ¼" (.5 cm) holes at the top through both layers, thread a ribbon through, and tie a bow.

Patchwork Quilt Card

From the contrasting card stock, cut thirteen 1" (3 cm) squares (twelve for the card and one for the envelope). Measure and lightly sketch in a 1" (3 cm) grid on surface of the purchased card. Glue the contrasting card stock squares to every other square on the grid to create a checkerboard pattern. Let dry. Use a fine-tip marking pen to draw tiny dashed lines near the edges of each square to simulate quilting. Glue the remaining square diagonally over the edge of the envelope as a seal.

Variation

This birth announcement is a variation on the "Bonjour!" card. Even though it looks totally different, it actually contains many of the same components in different colors. Use circle punches in several smaller sizes to add the pink paw pads, the facial details, and the tiny bear appliqué on the bib. Use heart punches in two sizes to the cut the pink muzzle and the ear linings. Underneath the balloon, glue on a 4" (10 cm) length of white cotton string. Use the photograph as a guide when selecting punches and placing the various elements on the card. Personalize the message in the balloon as you desire.

Snuggie Baby T-Shirt Card

Place the baby T-shirt template (page 119) on the card stock and trace around it with a pencil. Cut out the T-shirt shape on the marked outline. Fold up the bottom flap for a three-dimensional effect. Use a fine-tip marking pen to draw tiny dashed lines around the neckline, shoulders, and legs to simulate seams. Draw snaps and stitches along the curved edge of the folded-up flap. Print the baby's name and birth statistics on the front of the shirt.

Our Family Faces

Soft Picture Book

IT'S NEVER TOO EARLY *to introduce your baby to the joy of books. A lifetime of knowledge, adventure, and experience awaits the child who loves to read. And although your new arrival may not be ready for Dickens, any infant will be thrilled to hold this soft fabric volume—his very own, his very first, book. As a craft project, this baby book is simple enough for an older school-age sibling to make using her own artwork. An aunt might enjoy making baby's first counting book, or grandma could collect family photos for a first family album. Whatever the subject of your book, the technique is the same. Use inkjet-printable fabric sheets and your computer to create the pages. For more information on printable fabric images, see pages 16–17.*

Materials:

Two 8½" x 11" (22 cm x 28 cm) sheets of inkjet-printable fabric

Two 4" x 8" (10 cm x 20 cm) pieces of quilt batting

Matching sewing thread

Computer with inkjet printer

Sewing machine

Iron

Hand sewing needle, or ¼"-wide (.5 cm-wide) fusible tape

Pins

Air-soluble marking pen

Instructions

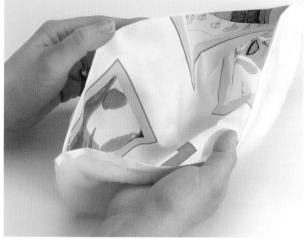

1. Choose and retrieve eight images from a computer scanner, digital camera, or e-mail function. Format four images using the greeting card template of a graphics program. Run a test on print paper. Mark ¼" (.5 cm) seam allowances as shown and confirm the alignment. Do a color printout on a fabric sheet. Repeat the process with four more images for the book's interior pages.

2. Press the two longer edges of the cover sheet ¼" (.5 cm) to the wrong side. Fold the sheet in half lengthwise, right side in. Pin a piece of batting underneath. Machine-stitch along the short edges, using ¼" (.5 cm) seam allowances. Clip the corners, turn right side out, and press. Slip-stitch the lower edge closed, or fuse the edges together using ¼" (.5 cm) fusible tape. Prepare the sheet with the book's inside pages the same way.

A Word About
Reading with Baby

Gather your baby in your lap for a cozy, quiet time as you explore each page of this little book together. The pleasant time you spend together will instill in the baby a love of reading that will continue throughout childhood.

3. To create a spine for the book, stitch two parallel lines ½" (1 cm) apart down the middle of the cover unit. Fold the unit with book's inside pages in half, so that the centerfold pictures are facing one another. Stitch close to the fold to create a small tuck. The slight reduction in page size will help the pages fit better within the cover.

4. To assemble the book, lay the cover unit flat, and place the inside pages on top. Make sure that the pages are in the correct sequence and that the images are all face up. Stitch two parallel lines ⅜" (1 cm) apart through the middle of the book though all the layers.

Variation

Use computer graphics to personalize a grown-up's book, too. Design your image using photos and graphics, print it onto inkjet-printable fabric, and then fuse it onto a fabric album cover.

Baby's Delights

Feast your eyes, feed your soul, feather your nest! The projects in this last section are designed to inspire you. There are guidelines and tips to accompany each one, but for the most part, your imagination will play a big part in determining the outcome. You can select the colors, textures, and amount of detail to suit your own crafting preferences and time frame.

The craft techniques used cover a wide range: decoupage, painting, sewing, cross-stitch, computer crafting—even something old into something new. Choose from our adorable little decoupage bookends, or perhaps a couple of fun painting projects—the comb and brush set or the colorful picture frame. Our sewing projects range from the simplest ducks-in-a-row crib hanger to a recycled linens-and-lace wall hanging and an heirloom cross-stitched quilt and pillow ensemble.

If new techniques in computer crafting appeal to you, capture baby's handprints on a decorative accent pillow. We've also included a whimsical no-sew Growth Chart to record baby's development over the years.

Whatever project you choose, you're bound to enjoy the creative process as well as the pleasure of seeing your finished work become part of the rich texture of a child's life.

Linens and Lace

Quilted Wall Hanging

A PERFECT WAY *to make use of antique table linens and heirloom lace that you have tucked away in a drawer is to incorporate them into a keepsake quilt or wall hanging. Textiles collected over the years or saved by family members can be brought together in a quilt that commemorates the birth of a new baby. This design was created by Janet Pensiero.*

Start with freshly laundered pieces of cotton or linen fabrics, such as a small tablecloth, linen napkins, or decorative pillowcases. Sew the pieces together to assemble the quilt top. Arrange pieces of crochet or lace strategically to cover any worn spots or discoloration. They can be attached by hand or machine. For an easy finish, pin the quilt top to a pale solid-color linen backing, right sides together, add a layer of batting, and stitch all around, leaving an opening for turning. Clip the corners and turn right side out so the batting is sandwiched in between. Slip-stitch to close the opening. Add antique mother-of-pearl buttons, stitching through all the layers for a tufted look.

A Word About

Safety

Use a quilt that's embellished with lace and buttons as a lap throw or wall hanging or for a decorative purpose. It is not suitable for covering a baby.

Moon and Stars

Decoupage Bookends

DECOUPAGE IS AN EASY WAY *to turn ordinary bookends into something more whimsical for baby's nursery. Start with purchased novelty bookends from a local retail store. The set we chose featured a yellow crescent moon and a blue star, each on a white base. To dress them up, we applied little animal designs cut from sheets of specialty gift wrap. If the images are too big, you can reduce them mechanically at a copy center. Use decoupage medium and a foam brush to adhere the shapes onto the bookends in a random design. Embellish further with small star stickers in coordinating colors. To seal surface, use the same decoupage medium. Apply several coats, allowing each coat to dry thoroughly before you apply the next one.*

A Word About

A Happy Childhood

Before a child can learn to master her own environment, she must feel loved and secure. When you play and interact with your baby, you are providing the happiness and security that will be the springboard for her future development.

Lots of Dots

Comb and Brush Set

YOU CAN EASILY TRANSFORM *a plain plastic brush and comb set into a charming and useful gift that any new mom would love to receive. Just add the decorative accents using some easy dip-and-dot applicators and acrylic craft paint. The completed set makes a perfect token to tuck into a lovely basket brimming with baby toiletries.*

Pour a little bit of paint in your selected colors onto a foam plate. Dip the alphabet letter applicator into the paint and press onto the surface to be painted. Choose any combination of letters you like. To paint a matching design on a narrow area, like the spine of a comb, use the tapered handle end of an artist's paintbrush. Just dip the tip of the handle into the paint and touch it to the surface multiple times in succession to create a series of colored dots. Once the paint is completely dry, brush on a coat of matte varnish to seal the painted design.

A Word About

Dips and Dots

One of the easiest ways to create a decorative surface with paint is to dip the handle end of a paintbrush in a small amount of paint and then lightly touch it to the surface to create a series of little dimensional dots. Practice first on a piece of paper until you are able to continually reproduce the same size dot.

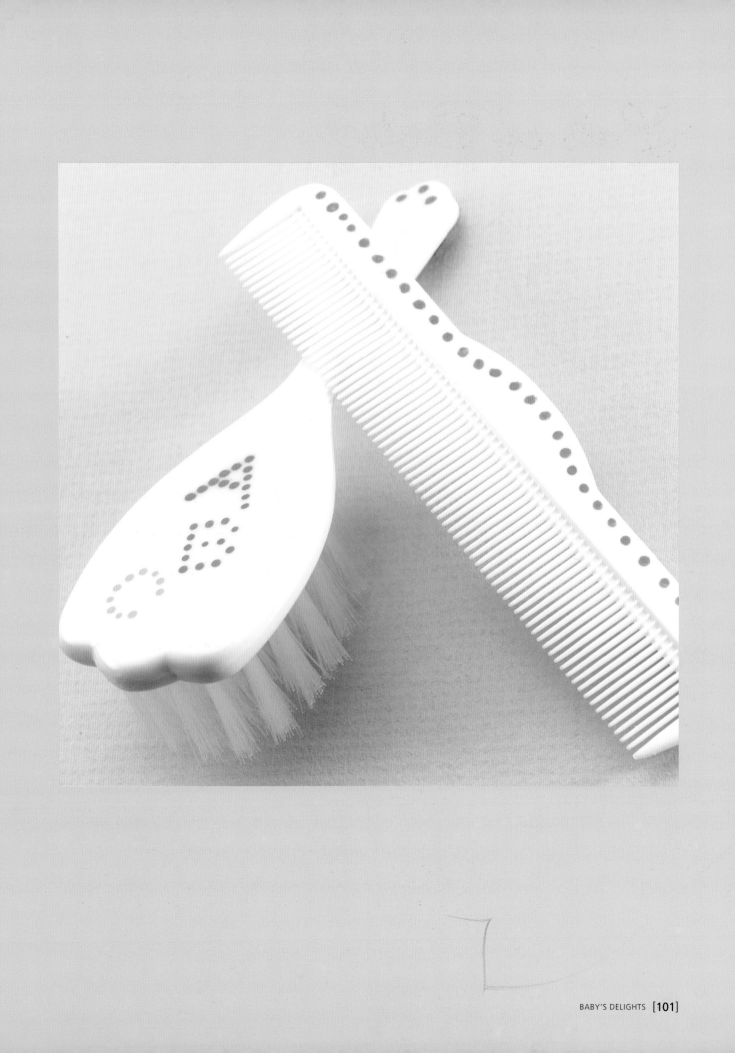

Picture Perfect

Painted Wooden Frame

THIS CHARMING ONE-OF-A-KIND *photo frame, created by Elizabeth Key Steverson, would make a sunny accent for any nursery décor. Start with a plain unfinished wooden frame, available in most craft stores. Use a foam brush to apply a base coat of orange acrylic craft paint. Let the paint dry completely, preferably one hour or longer. Apply the yellow paint with a novelty craft painting roller to create the gingham design. Attach purchased wooden accents with craft glue to complete the look. Your final step? Insert a picture of that adorable baby!*

A Word About

Novelty Paint Rollers and Sponges

You can achieve professional results with a craft paint roller in a fraction of the time it would take to paint with a brush. Craft rollers for creating stripes or plaids are available in several widths. Combine the stripes with colorful painted shapes created with sponge stamps for a whimsical, casual effect.

Ducks-in-a-Row

Hanging Crib Decor

THIS ADORABLE LITTLE SOFT HANGING *can add lots of stimulating color to a newborn's crib. We chose three colors of a whimsical ginghamlike print to coordinate our little flock of quackers. You could make a series of just about any simple animal shape, using the images in a children's coloring book or simple line drawings to make your patterns. Add ½" (1 cm) seam allowances all around, trace the patterns onto a double thickness of fabric, right sides facing, and cut out through both layers. Sew bills together, turn, and add a little batting to stuff. Arrange duck head between fabric layers and pin in place. Sew around duck leaving small opening at center of bottom to turn. Clip seams, trim points, and turn right side out. Stuff lightly and invisibly hand-sew closed. Sew circles for wheels and slit in center of one side to turn. Close the slit by hand and sew a coordinating button in the center of the other side of the circle to attach the wheel to the duck, covering the closure at the bottom of the duck. Add a smaller button for the eye. Sew the ducks together, bill to tail, to create "Ducks-in-a-Row." Attach a ribbon at each end to tie to a crib railing. NOTE: Be sure to remove this toy from the crib when baby begins to pull up, around five months.*

Hearts and Hands

Baby Handprint Pillow

CALL A HARDWORKING, FUN-LOVING FRIEND *for this next project, because it's definitely a two-person job. Design the face of the pillow with a computer graphics program, making sure to leave an empty spot for the handprints. Print the design on inkjet-printable fabric (pages 16–17); make several copies in case of runs, smears, or drips.*

Now comes the fun part. Mommy's job is simple: Hold the baby's hands and guide them to the fabric. Fun-loving friend's job is more complex: Apply nontoxic paint to baby's hands, hold the fabric steady, be ready with a damp cloth, keep baby happy, and take plenty of photographs. Sew the pillow cover when the paint is thoroughly dry.

A Word About

Babies and Paint

The math is simple: The less paint you put on baby, the less paint will end up on you, your clothes, the dog, and the walls. Wear old clothing, do one hand at a time and practice on paper if you feel the need. Using an artist's brush, apply the paint to baby's hand in a thin layer—remember, "less is more." Don't be discouraged if you get a good, clear print accompanied by a few blank spots. Just dab in some paint with your own finger to fill in the blank areas.

Marie
3/7/2001

Watch Me Grow

No-Sew Growth Chart

IT'S ALWAYS THE SAME OLD STORY. *After taking it easy for a while, babies suddenly seem to start crawling, standing, walking, and running. As soon as he stands, but before he runs out the door, start a record of your child's vertical progress. This playful "family tree" growth chart, made entirely of felt, has a fabric tape measure running down the middle of the tree trunk. Each apple bears a photo of your growing child, while the leaves pinpoint his height in inches. Simple patterns (page 123) and no-sew fusible adhesive make this a fast, easy project. If you're planning a big family, make enough apples in advance to accommodate your growing clan. As the years pass, the tree will stand as a vibrant record of all your children at various ages. You'll treasure it long after your last "baby" has left for college.*

A Word About

Hanging Your Growth Chart

Use a yardstick to measure up from the floor to the height of the lowest height measurement on the chart. Have someone help you hang the chart so that it is at the proper height for accurate measurement.

Heirloom Keepsake

Cross-Stitched Quilt and Pillow

THIS BEAUTIFUL ENSEMBLE *was created by well-known textile artist Elaine Schmidt. The multicolored patchwork gingham provides a pleasing backdrop for the cross-stitched alphabet letters and flowers blooming in each corner of the quilt. Multiple borders and bindings, embellished with variegated rickrack in coordinating pastels, frame the alphabet motifs. The matching pillow is embroidered with the child's name and birth date. A wide gingham ruffle and more rickrack complete the look. A project like this, that takes time and love to make, will always be treasured.*

A Word About

Gingham and Cross Stitch

Gingham provides the perfect grid upon which to create cross-stitch patterns. The white squares can be marked with an air-soluble pen to center your design in the quilt square. Use simple shapes from coloring books or draw block letters and numbers to create a personalized heirloom quilt for the new baby in your family.

Template Patterns

This section includes complete template patterns for all the sewing projects and two of the paper projects in this book. To make a template, you will need card stock or heavy clear acetate. Lay tracing paper over the pattern in the book and trace all the pattern markings. Transfer the markings to the card stock with transfer or carbon paper or by fusing. To mark acetate, simply lay the clear acetate sheet over the book pattern and use a permanent marking pen to trace the markings. If you have access to a photocopier, you can copy the patterns mechanically from the book directly onto card stock or acetate sheets. Carefully cut out each marked piece to complete the template.

The templates are used in different ways for different projects, so be sure to read all the project instructions completely before cutting into your fabric.

One shortcut for creating basic two-layer shapes (where the front and back pieces are exactly the same) is to cut a template to the exact shape of the finished piece without added seam allowances. Fold the fabric, right side in, to make a double layer. Lay the template on top, and trace around the outside edges to mark the exact stitching line. The pieces are sewn together before you cut them out. You'll notice that the pattern pieces for this method always include a "slit to turn" marking. Instead of leaving an opening in the stitched seam for turning, a slit is cut in the middle of one of the pieces after sewing. This technique preserves the integrity of the sewn shape; it works especially well with shapes that are small.

Some of the template patterns do include seam allowances. These stitching lines are clearly marked with a dashed line, usually ¼" (.5 cm) inside the cutting line. This method is used when dissimilar pieces must be sewn together or when special indicators are necessary.

Decorative Padded Hangers *(page 24)*

Flower

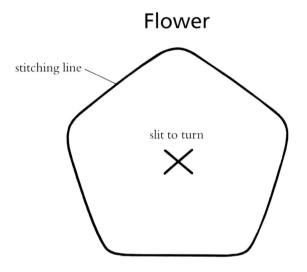

stitching line

slit to turn

Leaves

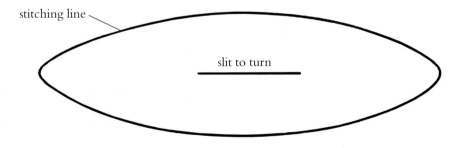

stitching line

slit to turn

photocopy this page at 100%

Cozy Baby Ensemble *(page 42)*

Peapod

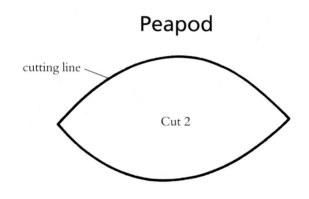

cutting line

Cut 2

photocopy this page at 100%

Appliqué Party Dress *(page 50)*

Heart

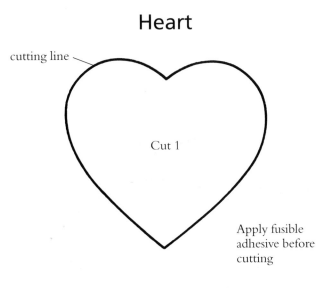

cutting line

Cut 1

Apply fusible
adhesive before
cutting

Star

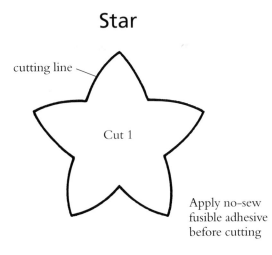

cutting line

Cut 1

Apply no-sew
fusible adhesive
before cutting

photocopy this page at 100%

Sweater Duck Family *(page 60)*

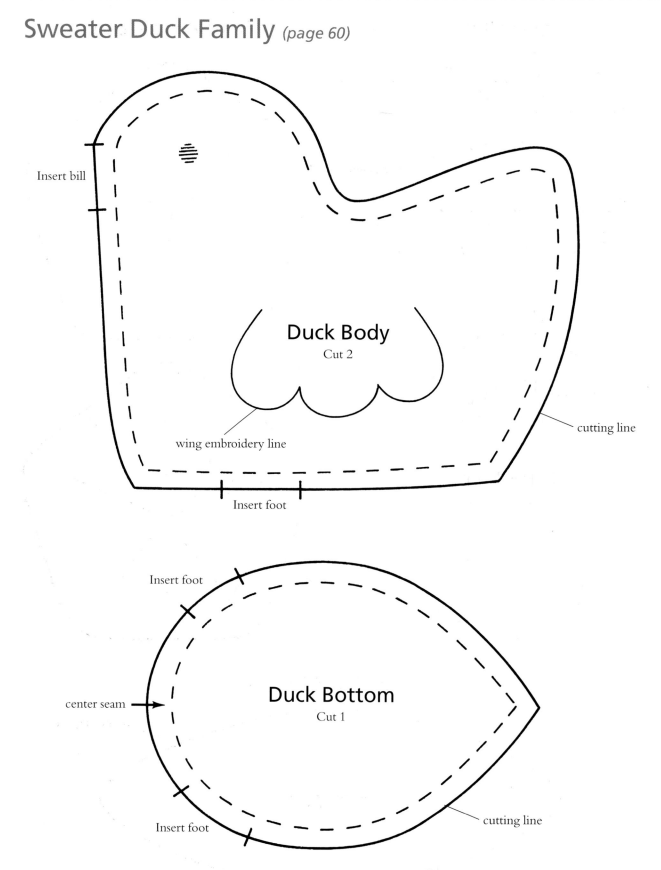

Insert bill

Duck Body
Cut 2

wing embroidery line

cutting line

Insert foot

Insert foot

center seam

Duck Bottom
Cut 1

Insert foot

cutting line

photocopy both pages at 100%

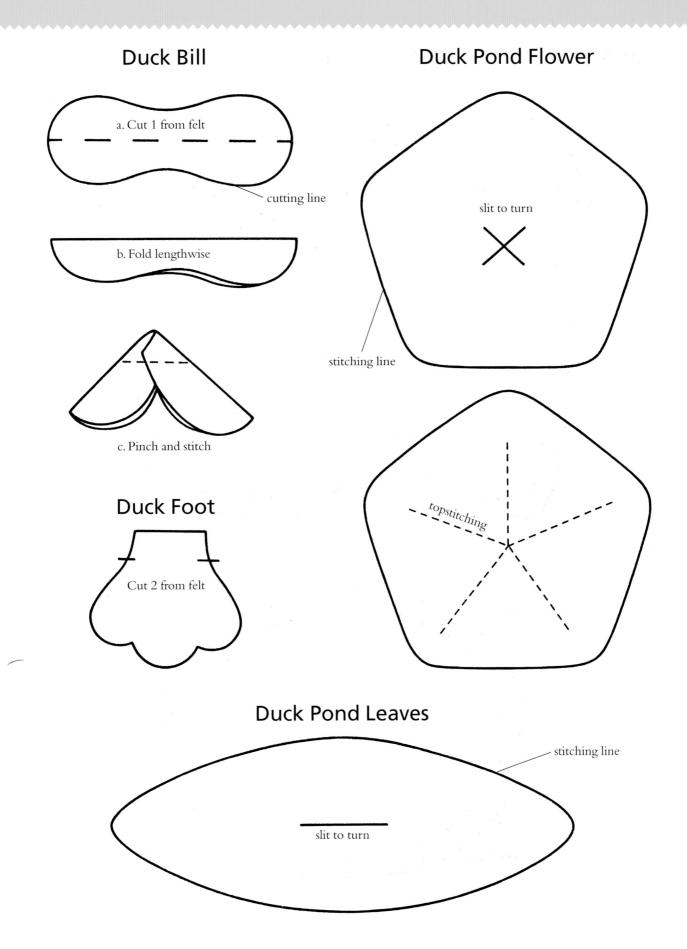

Duck Bill

a. Cut 1 from felt

cutting line

b. Fold lengthwise

c. Pinch and stitch

Duck Foot

Cut 2 from felt

Duck Pond Flower

slit to turn

stitching line

topstitching

Duck Pond Leaves

stitching line

slit to turn

Keepsake Birth Announcements *(page 86)*

Bib Card

cutting line for Ruffle Template
cutting line for Bib Template
cutting line for Ruffle Template
Double-Sided
Adhesive Ring
Use both templates to mark this narrow ring. Mark the inside line first.

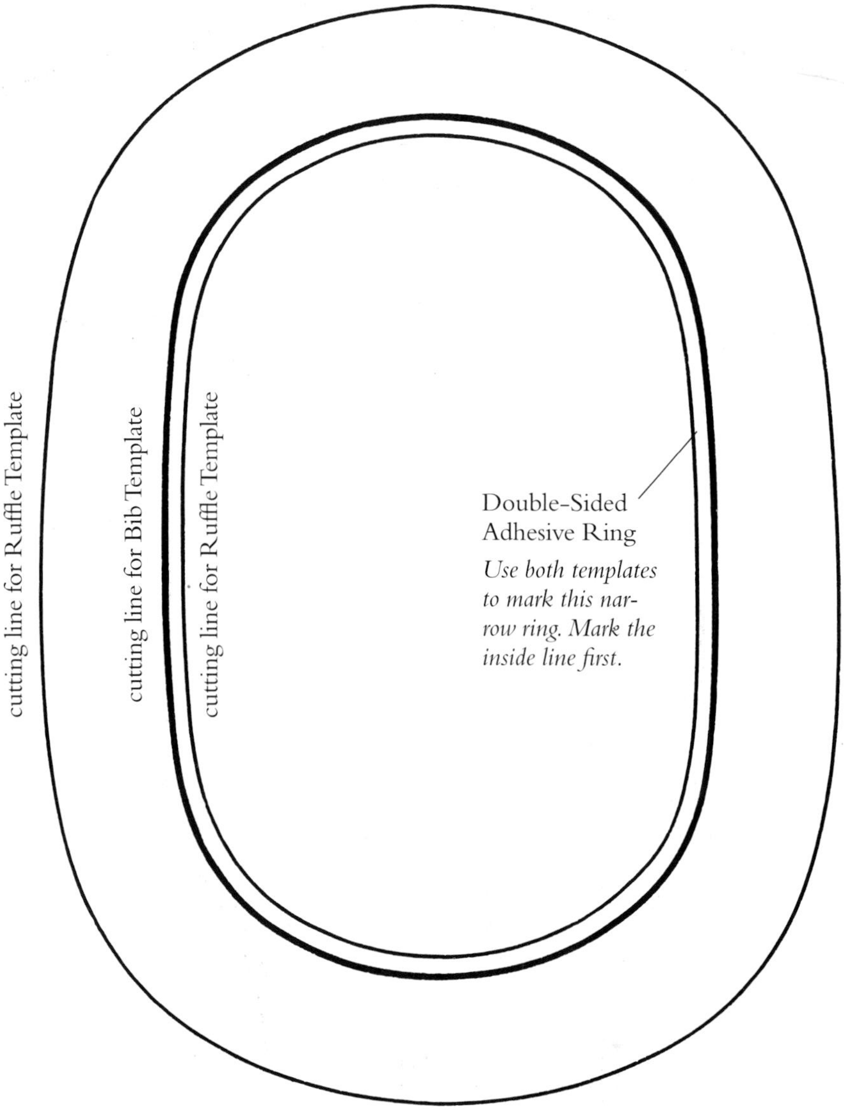

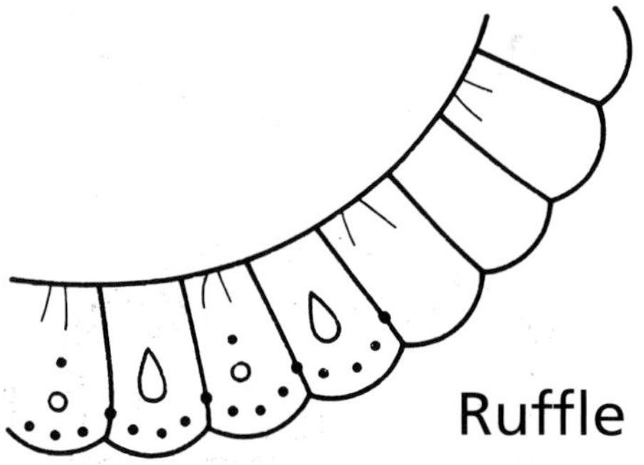

Ruffle Diagram

photocopy this page at 125%

T-Shirt Card

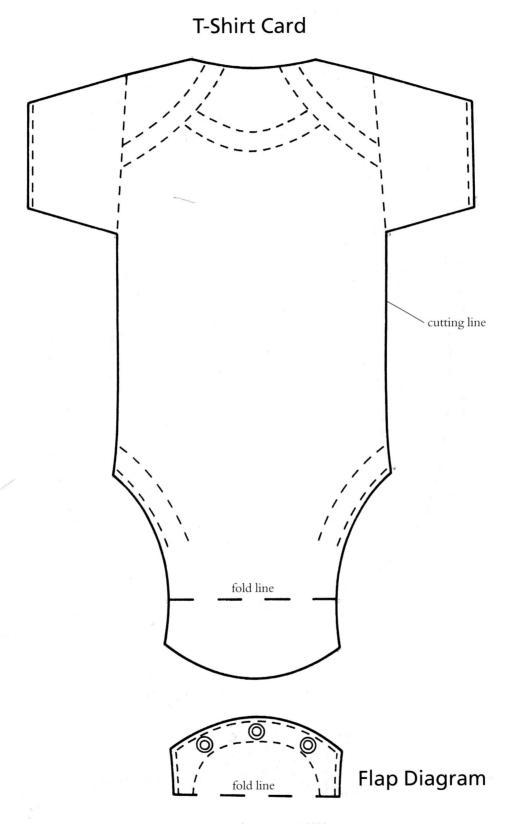

cutting line

fold line

fold line

Flap Diagram

photocopy this page at 100%

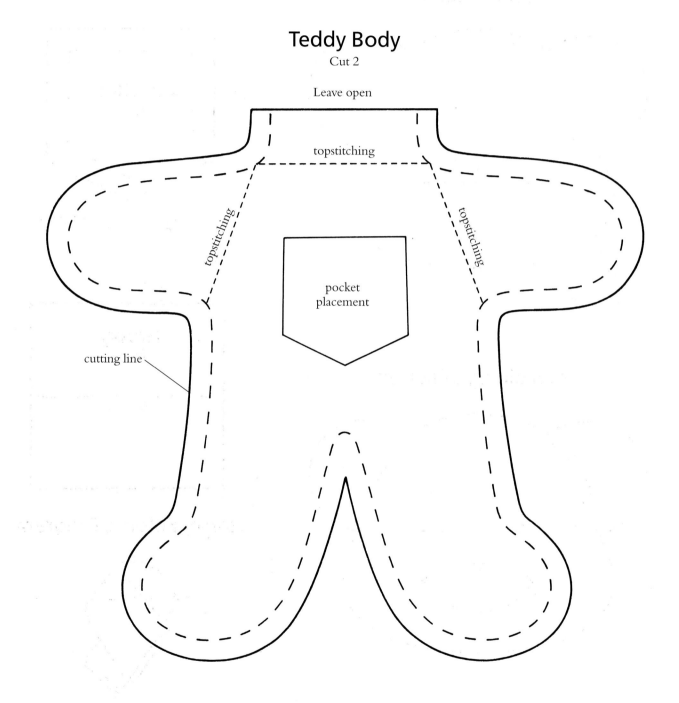

Teddy Body
Cut 2

Leave open

topstitching

topstitching

topstitching

pocket
placement

cutting line

photocopy this page at 118%

Teddy Head

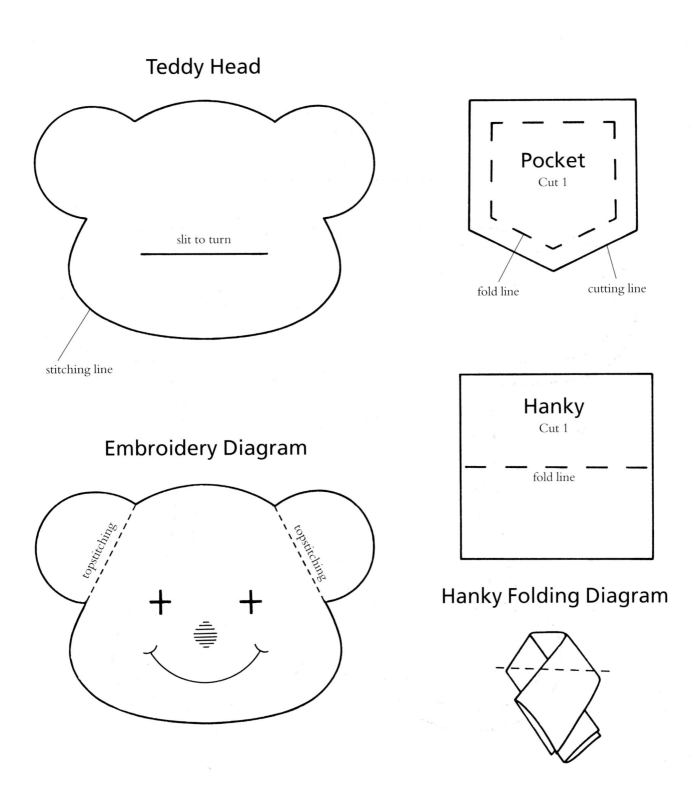

slit to turn

stitching line

Pocket
Cut 1

fold line   cutting line

Embroidery Diagram

topstitching   topstitching

Hanky
Cut 1

fold line

Hanky Folding Diagram

photocopy this page at 118%

Bear Head

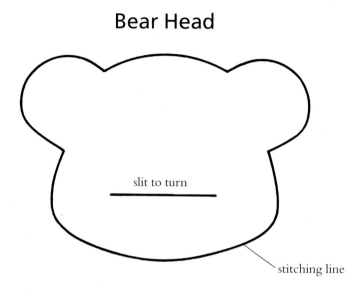

slit to turn

stitching line

Embroidery Diagram

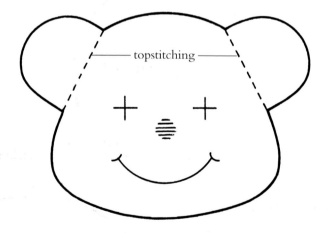

topstitching

photocopy this page at 100%

No-Sew Growth Chart *(page 108)*

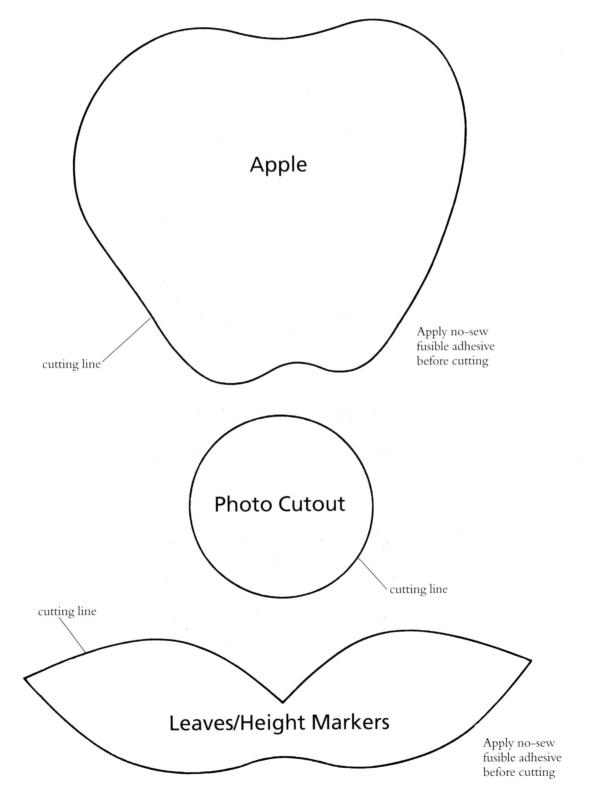

Apple

cutting line

Apply no-sew
fusible adhesive
before cutting

Photo Cutout

cutting line

cutting line

Leaves/Height Markers

Apply no-sew
fusible adhesive
before cutting

photocopy this page at 118%

Product Resource Guide

This guide is organized both by project and by vendor. Look under the project name to find out more about the particular products and materials used. For further information, or to purchase a product, consult the vendor listing that follows.

Baby's Room

page 24
Decorative Padded Hangers
   Foam pipe insulation from Home Depot.
   Polyfil® polyester fiberfill and batting from Fairfield Processing, Inc.
   Velvet tubing from Wright's.
   Air-soluble marker from EZ International.

page 28
Painted Wooden Letters
   5" wooden letters from Hobby Lobby retail craft stores.
   Decorating stylus from NSI.
   Decor-it! paints from NSI.

page 32
Nursery Lamp Shade
   Self-adhesive lamp shade from Hollywood Lights.
   Kunin® felt from The Fabric Club.
   Giant chenille rickrack from Wright's.
   Colorfast inkjet printable fabric sheets from June Tailor.
   HeatNBond® Ultrahold fusible adhesive from Therm O Web.
   Crafter's Pick "The Ultimate"® adhesive from API.
   Air-soluble marker from EZ International.

page 36
Musical Crib Mobile
   Crib mobile arm and musical turning mechanism from Judi's Originals.
   Felt craft sheets available in most craft and fabric stores.
   Plastic foam balls from Syndicate Sales.
   Giant chenille rickrack, chenille cord from Wright's.
   Crafter's Pick "The Ultimate"® adhesive from API.
   White Folk Art acrylic craft paint from Plaid.

Baby's Clothes and Comforts

page 42
Cozy Baby Ensemble
   Cotton flannel fabric from The Fabric Club.
   Air-soluble marker from EZ International.

page 46
Cuddly Activity Blanket
   Fleece fabric from The Fabric Club.
   HeatNBond Lite® sewable fusible adhesive from Therm O Web.
   Giant chenille rickrack from Wright's.
   Plastic attachment rings from New Baby Products.

page 50
Appliqué Party Dress
   HeatNBond Lite® sewable fusible adhesive, HeatNBond Ultra-Hold® no-sew fusible adhesive from Therm O Web.
   Air-soluble marker from EZ International.

page 54
Knitted Cap and Booties
   Yarn, needles, ring markers from Patternworks.

Baby's Toys

page 60
Sweater Duck Family
   Tapestry yarn from DMC.
   Velvet ribbon from Wright's.
   Fusible tricot from HTC.
   Fleece fabric from The Fabric Club.
   Polyfil® quilt batting from Fairfield Processing, Inc.
   Velcro® Soft Touch® hook-and-loop fastener.

page 64
Teddy Bear Wrist Rattle
   Fleece fabric from The Fabric Club.
   Small plastic rattle insert from National Artcraft.
   Velcro® hook-and-loop fastener.
   Polyfil® Polyester fiberfill from Fairfield Processing, Inc.
   Embroidery floss from DMC.
   Air-soluble marker from EZ International.

page 68
Stuffed Fabric Blocks
   Polyfil® Polyester fiberfill from Fairfield Processing, Inc.
   Air-soluble marker from EZ International.

page 72
Denim Teddy Bear
   Air-soluble marker from EZ International.
   Polyfil® Polyester fiberfill from Fairfield Processing, Inc.
   Embroidery floss from DMC.

Baby's Memories

page 78
Clay-and-Wire Photo Holder
   Fimo Soft® polymer clay, teddy bear push mold, Nu Blade® polymer clay slicing blade from American Art Clay Company.
   Crafter's Pick "The Ultimate"® adhesive from API.
   22-gauge armature wire from Dick Blick.
   Beads from The Beadery

page 82
Photo Memory Album
   Crafter's Pick "The Ultimate"® adhesive from API.
   Polyfil® Extra Loft quilt batting from Fairfield Processing, Inc.
   Grosgrain ribbon from Wright's.

page 86
Keepsake Birth Announcements
   Vellums and specialty papers by DMD
   Keep-A-Memory double-sided adhesive from Therm O Web.
   Punches and decorative edge scissors from Emagination Crafts.
   Crafter's Pick "The Ultimate"® adhesive from API.

page 90
Soft Picture Book
   Colorfast inkjet-printable fabric sheets from June Tailor.
   Polyfil® quilt batting from Fairfield Processing, Inc.
   Air-soluble marker from EZ International.
   HeatNBond Quilter's Choice fusible adhesive tape from Therm O Web.

Baby's Delights

page 96
Quilted Wall Hanging
  Polyfil® quilt batting from
  Fairfield Processing, Inc.

page 98
Decoupage Bookends
  Restore & Restyle Kids
  "Stars & Moons Collec-
  tions" bookends from Target.
  Wrapping paper with whim-
  sical design from Sam Flax.
  RoyalCoat decoupage
  medium from Plaid.

page 100
Comb and Brush Set
  Fun to Paint Alphabet
  Dotters, Folk Art acrylic
  paint, acrylic matte varnish
  from Plaid.

page 102
Painted Wooden Frame
  Crafty Productions Inc.
  "Stop & Smell the Roses"
  frame, Folk Art acrylic paint,
  Fun to Paint stripe roller
  from Plaid.
  Handmade Creations deco-
  rative wooden shapes by Per-
  leberg available at JoAnn's.
  Crafter's Pick "The Ulti-
  mate"® adhesive by API.

page 104
Hanging Crib Decor
  Polyfil® Polyester fiberfill
  from Fairfield Processing, Inc.

page 106
Baby Handprint Pillow
  Colorfast inkjet-printable
  fabric sheets from June Tailor.
  Polyfil® Polyester fiberfill
  from Fairfield Processing, Inc.
  Folk Art acrylic craft paint
  from Plaid.

page 108
No-Sew Growth Chart
  Colorfast inkjet-printable
  fabric sheets from June Tailor.
  Kunin® felt from The
  Fabric Club.
  HeatNBond Ultra® no-sew
  fusible adhesive from Therm
  O Web.

page 110
Cross-Stitched Quilt
and Pillow
  Polyfil® Polyester fiberfill
  from Fairfield Processing, Inc.
  Polyfil® Extra Loft quilt
  batting from Fairfield
  Processing, Inc.
  Embroidery floss from DMC.

Vendors/Manufacturers

American Art Clay Co.
(317) 244-6871
www.amaco.com
4717 W. 16th Street
Indianapolis, IN 46222

API-Crafters Pick
(510) 526-7616
www.crafterspick.com
520 Cleveland Avenue
Albany, CA 94710

The Beadery
(401) 539-2432
www.the beadery.com
PO Box 178
105 Canonchet Road
Hope Valley, RI 02832

The DMC Corporation
(973) 589-0606
www.dmc-usa.com
South Hackensack Avenue
Port Kearny, Building 10A
South Kearny, NJ 07032

DMD Industries
(501) 750-8929
www.dmdind.com
1205 ESI Drive
Springdale, AR 72764

Dick Blick Art Materials
(800) 828-4548
www.dickblick.com
PO Box 1267
Galesburg, IL 61401-1267

Emagination Crafts Inc.
(630) 238-9770
www.emaginationcrafts.com
530 N. York Road
Bensenville, IL 60106

The Fabric Club
(800) 322-2582
www.fabricclub.com
PO Box 767670
Roswell, GA 30078

Fairfield Processing Corp.
(800) 980-8000
www.poly-fil.com
88 Rose Hill Avenue
PO Box 1130
Danbury, CT 06813

HTC Inc.
(973) 618-9380
www.htc-inc.net
103 Eisenhower Parkway
Rosland, NJ 07068

Judi's Originals
Available at juvenile
specialty stores

June Tailor, Inc.
(800) 844-5400 for retail
locations
www.junetailor.com
PO Box 208
2861 Highway 175
Richfield, WI 53076-0208

National Artcraft
(888) 937-2723
www.nationalartcraft.com
7996 Darrow Road
Twinsburg, OH 44087

NSI
(516) 678-1700
www.decoritpaint.com
910 Orlando Avenue
West Hempstead, NY
  11552-3942

Patternworks
(800) 438-5464
www.patternworks.com
PO Box 1690
Poughkeepsie, NY 12601-0690

Plaid Enterprises, Inc.
(678) 291-8100
www.plaidonline.com
3225 Westech Drive
Norcross, GA 30092

Restore & Restyle Kids
Available at Target

Sam Flax
(212) 620-3038
12 West 20th Street
New York, NY 10011

Syndicate Sales
(765) 457-7277
www.syndicatesales.com
2025 N. Wabash Street
PO Box 756
Kokomo, IN 46903-0756

Therm O Web
(847) 520-5200
www.thermoweb.com
770 Glenn Avenue
Wheeling, IL 60090

William E. Wright Ltd.
Partnership
(800) 628-9362
www.wrights.com
85 South Street
PO Box 398
West Warren, MA 01092

Wisconsin Lighting, Inc.
(715) 834-8707
www.wilighting.com
800 Wisconsin Street
Suite D02-104
Eau Claire, WI 54703

*All the sewn projects in this book
were created on a Viking Designer
1 sewing machine. For more information on this machine and other
Viking products, contact:*

Viking Sewing Machines, Inc.
(440) 808-6711
www.husqvarnaviking.com
31000 Viking Parkway
Westlake OH 44145-8012

Contributors

Debra Kahn
2084 DeKalb Avenue
Atlanta, GA 30307
phone: (404) 371-8211
Debra Kahn knitted the cap, booties, and bib. She specializes in one-of-a-kind knitted pieces.

Sonny Knox
Grand Manors
3735 Poplar Drive
Clarkston, GA 30021
phone: (404) 292-2207
sonnyknox@mindspring.com
Sonny Knox crafted the image transfer projects and the crib mobile. He is a graphic designer and multimedia artist.

Sally O. Lee
35 Locust Street, Unit 5
Danvers, MA 01923
phone and fax: (978) 762-0097
sallyolee@aol.com
Sally Lee designed the patchwork quilt and baby T-shirt cards. She is an illustrator for several magazines, children's books, and various other commissions.

Gloria Bell Parker
Bell Parker Designs
708 Killian Street #2
Atlanta, GA 30312
phone: (404) 635-1696
Gloria Bell Parker crafted the padded hangers, wrist rattle, sweater ducks, denim teddies, appliqué dress, and activity blanket. She is a quilt and textile artist.

Janet Pensiero
263 Dupont Street
Philadelphia, PA 19128
phone and fax: (215) 487-2553
janetpensiero@gateway.net
Janet Pensiero designed the recycled linens and lace quilt. She is a designer working in a variety of craft media.

Vivian Peritts
Vivian's Originals
763 Dover Street
Marietta, GA 30060
phone and fax: (770) 926-4568
VPeritts@aol.com
Vivian Peritts designed the punched paper birth announcements. She is a designer working in all craft media.

Elaine Schmidt
Elaine Schmidt Designs
21 Sierra Drive
Califon, NJ 07830
phone: (908) 832-2222
fax: (908) 832-9108
ESDesigns@aol.com
Elaine Schmidt designed the cross-stitched quilt and keepsake pillow. She is a textile artist and multimedia craft designer.

Elizabeth Key Steverson
522 Gregg Drive
Lilburn, GA 30047
phone and fax: (770) 806-2286
EKS5220@aol.com
Elizabeth Key Steverson crafted the wire photo holder, photo albums and frame, comb and brush set, painted wooden letters, and decoupage bookends. She is an artist.

Acknowledgments

I would like to thank the following crafters and designers who generously lent their time, skills, and considerable talents to the projects in this book: Debra Kahn, Sonny Knox, Gloria Bell Parker, Janet Pensiero, Vivian Peritts, Cheryl Runyan, Elaine Schmidt, Elizabeth Key Steverson.

Thanks to Shawna Mullen, Mary Ann Hall, Martha Wetherill, and Candie Frankel at Rockport Publishers for the opportunity and assistance in making this project come together.

Also, thanks to Samantha Lill, for modeling the knitwear and wrist rattle, and her mom, Janine.

Finally, special thanks to Sonny Knox and Lambert Greene for lending support to the project way beyond the call of duty, including eleventh-hour trips to FedEx and emergency computer resuscitation. Thanks, Guys—couldn't have done it without you!

About the Author

Lynne Farris is a fabric artist, professional designer, and frequent guest on HGTV and the Discovery Channel. She was trained as a visual artist, began her career as a college art instructor, and then worked for several years in product development in the toy and juvenile products industries. Her work is often published in leading craft magazines, and she works as a creative and marketing consultant to several leading manufacturers.

Owner of Lynne Farris Gallery, she is active in the local arts community in Atlanta, Georgia.

Lynne Farris Designs
50 Hurt Plaza, Suite 105
Atlanta, GA 30303
(404) 688-7311
lynnefarris@msn.com
www.lynnefarris.com